LETTING
GOD
BLESS
YOU

LETTING
GOD
BLESS
YOU

The Beatitudes for Today

JOHN KILLINGER

Abingdon Press
Nashville

LETTING GOD BLESS YOU
THE BEATITUDES FOR TODAY

This book is printed on recycled, acid-free paper.

Library of Congress Cataloging-in-Publication Data

Killinger, John
   Letting God bless you : the beatitudes for today / by John Killinger.
     p. cm. -- (Killinger for today.)
   ISBN 0-687-21569-2
   1. Beatitudes. I. Title. II. Series.
BT382.K55 1993   92-11245
241.5'3—dc20   CIP

Scripture quotations, unless otherwise noted, are from the New Revised Standard Version of the Bible, copyright 1989 by the Division of Christian Education of the National Council of the Churches of Christ in the USA. Used by permission.

Scripture quotations marked RSV are from the Revised Standard Version of the Bible copyright 1946, 1952, 1971 by the Division of Christian Education of the National Council of the Churches of Christ in the USA. Used by permission.

Scripture quotations marked NJB are from the New Jerusalem Bible. Copyright 1985 by Darton, Longman & Todd, Ltd. and Doubleday & Company, Inc.

Scripture quotations marked KJV are from the King James version of the Bible.

MANUFACTURED IN THE UNITED STATES OF AMERICA

For Charlotte Baughn,
who fills our lives
with sunshine and flowers

CONTENTS

INTRODUCTION

There have been many epoch-making events in the history of the world—the legalization of Christianity in A.D. 313, the fall of Rome in A.D. 476, the Norman Conquest of England in A.D. 1066, the printing of the first book on the Gutenberg press in A.D. 1453, the discovery of America in A.D. 1492, the definitive beginning of the Protestant Reformation in A.D. 1517, the American Revolution in A.D. 1776, the use of a steam engine to power a cotton mill in A.D. 1785, the publication of Darwin's *Origin of the Species* in A.D. 1859, the unveiling of atomic force in A.D. 1945—but only one event has ever divided all history into two parts, and that is the birth of Jesus Christ.

It was the importance of this birth, and the sheer enormity of the importance, that led the man whom we know as Matthew to write an account of Jesus' life, beginning not with the birth itself but with the entire prehistory of the world as the Jews understood it, all the way back to their father Abraham, and demonstrating that all those years, significant as they were, were merely a prelude to the coming of the Christ. That coming alone split everything into *before* and *after*.

E. Stanley Jones, the great Methodist missionary, tells in his autobiography *A Song of Ascents* about an African who, following his conversion, changed his name to "After." Everything he considered important in his life happened after he met Christ. Jones said it was this way in his own life (Nashville: Abingdon Press, 1968, p. 16).

And Matthew evidently felt the same way. What drama he therefore saw in the symphony of events surrounding the actual birth of Jesus!

First there was the extraordinary conception of the Christ child in his mother's womb—extraordinary because it was not from his future father's sperm but by the power of the Spirit of God.

Then there was the visit of an angel, who appeared to the earthly father in a dream and told him the child was a miracle child who would save his people from their sins.

Next, an international ingredient was added to the story. Astrologers from the Far East appeared in Jerusalem, inquiring about the birth of the child they called "king of the Jews." This deepened the intrigue, for it alerted the degenerate King Herod to a future threat to his throne. He ordered the astrologers to bring him news if they found the baby.

They found the baby and his parents, but then, like the baby's father, had a dream filled with meaning. They were not to tell Herod what they knew, but to return home without revisiting Jerusalem. The baby's father, meanwhile, had another angelic visit in a dream, warning him to flee with the child into Egypt. Herod, outwitted, fell into a rage and ordered all male children in the land under two years of age to be callously slain. There was great outrage and grieving in the whole realm.

Once more, when Herod died, the angel appeared to the baby's father in a dream and told him it was safe to return to their homeland. Yet another dream cautioned him about settling in the area around Jerusalem and directed that he take the child and his mother northward into Galilee. Thus the child was reared as a Nazarene.

Several years later. Enter John the Baptist, a popular ascetic preacher dwelling in the wilderness and calling the people of Israel to repentance. Jesus, now a young man, traveled down from Galilee to seek baptism by John. When John saw him, some spiritual intuition led him to demur. "I need to be baptized by you," he said, "and do you come to me?" (Matt. 3:14). But Jesus persuaded him and was baptized. Immediately the heavens rumbled. The Spirit of God descended in the form of a dove and lit upon him. There was a voice from the skies, saying, "This is my Son, the Beloved, with whom I am well pleased" (Matt. 3:17).

Like young warriors in ancient myths and stories, Jesus entered the wilderness for forty days and nights to be tested by the Evil One. The temptations were dramatic. Psychologists would call them hallucinative, involving great heights, panoramic views, and unbelievable offers if he would renounce his heavenly mission. But he remained faithful to the end, and at last the angels came and ministered to his fatigued spirit and weary body.

But the Evil One was not through. Maybe the Son of God had withstood his wiles, but he could still make his terrible power felt in the land. Poor John the Baptist was arrested by Herod's soldiers and thrown into prison, where he would languish for months, his followers in defeat and disarray. Eventually John's head would be brought to Herod on a silver platter, victim of an orgiastic whim and the undiminished strength of the Evil One.

We are so familiar with the story, have heard it told and preached so many times, that it has lost its edge with us. But not so to Matthew or the people who lived in an age of storytelling, when every bush and brook was thought to be alive with the spirit of some foul or friendly demon. For Matthew, it was high drama, the very stuff of deep, immortal conflict. Here was the watershed of the ages! Jesus was the hero of eternity, sent by God to enjoin the Evil One in a contest for the souls of human beings. The various stories—of a miraculous birth, angels appearing in dreams, Wise Men from the East, the slaughter of the innocents, the death of John the Baptist—were all signs of the hideous warfare. Darkness and light were locked in combat! Even if the events described occurred in a small, nondescript country of little consequence in the general history of the world, the events themselves were anything but small, nondescript, and without consequence. On the contrary, they were events that would define life on the entire planet for all time to come, even for time beyond time. They were events of cosmic consequence, of indescribable significance. Even secular historians with no passion for religious affairs would be forced to date their annals from this single most cataclysmic occurrence in the life of the world.

Jesus had come with the reign of God.

What did it mean for God's rule to come on earth? For centuries, the prophetic tradition in Israel had prepared the people of that little nation to expect a day when God would overthrow all faithless, despotic earthly rulers and take their thrones himself. The author of 1 Chronicles represented the prophet Nathan as delivering this message from God to David, the king:

> When your days are fulfilled to go to be with your ancestors, I will raise up your offspring after you, one of your own sons, and I will establish his kingdom. He shall build a house for me, and I will establish his throne forever. I will be a father to him, and he shall be a son to me. I will not take my steadfast love from him, as I took it from him who was before you, but I will confirm him in my house and in my kingdom forever, and his throne shall be established forever. (1 Chron. 17:11-14)

Several of the psalms, the devotional literature of Israel, pictured God as enthroned above all earthly rulers, immune to the desolation he would one day wreak among enemies and unbelievers:

> God is our refuge and strength,
>   a very present help in trouble.
> Therefore we will not fear, though the earth should change,
>   though the mountains shake in the heart of the sea;
> though its waters roar and foam,
>   though the mountains tremble with its tumult.
>
> There is a river whose streams make glad the city of God,
>   the holy habitation of the Most High.
> God is in the midst of the city; it shall not be moved;
>   God will help it when the morning dawns.
> The nations are in an uproar, the kingdoms totter;
>   he utters his voice, the earth melts.
> The LORD of hosts is with us;
>   the God of Jacob is our refuge.
>
> (Ps. 46:1-7)

> Say among the nations, "The LORD is king!
>   The world is firmly established; it shall never be moved.
>   He will judge the peoples with equity."
> Let the heavens be glad, and let the earth rejoice;
>   let the sea roar, and all that fills it;
>   let the field exult, and everything in it.

12

Then shall all the trees of the forest sing for joy
    before the LORD; for he is coming,
    for he is coming to judge the earth.
He will judge the world with righteousness,
    and the peoples with his truth.

                                        (Ps. 96:10-13)

Make a joyful noise to the LORD, all the earth;
    break forth into joyous song and sing praises.
Sing praises to the LORD with the lyre,
    with the lyre and the sound of melody.
With trumpets and the sound of the horn
    make a joyful noise before the King, the LORD.
(Ps. 98:4-6)

The LORD is king; let the peoples tremble!
    He sits enthroned upon the cherubim; let the earth quake!
The LORD is great in Zion;
    he is exalted over all the peoples.
Let them praise your great and awesome name!
    Holy is he!
Mighty King, lover of justice,
    you have established equity;
you have executed justice
    and righteousness in Jacob.
Extol the LORD our God;
    worship at his footstool.
    Holy is he!

                                        (Ps. 99:1-5)

    The prophets foresaw a day when God would fulfill his
promises by scattering his enemies, occupying a throne in Judah,
and bringing justice and peace in all the world. Thus this beautiful passage from Isaiah:

        The people who walked in darkness
            have seen a great light;
        those who lived in a land of deep darkness—
            on them light has shined.

You have multiplied the nation,
　you have increased its joy;
they rejoice before you
　as with joy at the harvest,
　as people exult when dividing plunder.
For the yoke of their burden,
　and the bar across their shoulders,
　the rod of their oppressor,
　you have broken as on the day of Midian.
For all the boots of the tramping warriors
　and all the garments rolled in blood
　shall be burned as fuel for the fire.
For a child has been born for us,
　a son given to us;
authority rests upon his shoulders;
　and he is named
Wonderful Counselor, Mighty God,
　Everlasting Father, Prince of Peace.
His authority shall grow continually,
　and there shall be endless peace
for the throne of David and his kingdom.
　He will establish and uphold it
with justice and with righteousness
　from this time onward and forevermore.
The zeal of the LORD of hosts will do this.

(Isa. 9:2-7)

T. Urban Holmes, once dean of the School of Theology of the University of the South, was fond of referring to this idealistic rule of God as the reign of "the anti-structure." When God fulfilled the divine promises to Israel, the worldly structures would be overthrown—evil, injustice, poverty, hunger, the sway of tyrants—and their opposites would be enthroned. Goodness would predominate, justice would roll down like waters, poverty and hunger would disappear before the sharing of earth's bounties, and God alone would be monarch of the empires, a ruler above all rulers.

Little wonder that this prospect was daunting to the uneasy despots of Jesus' day, or that Herod (and later Caesar) would see in the loyalty of the Nazarene's followers a threat to his own security on the throne. W. H. Auden, in his Christmas oratorio *For the Time Being,* has caught the flavor of Herod's thinking after he learned of the birth of Christ:

> Today, apparently, judging by the trio who came to see me this morning with an ecstatic grin on their scholarly faces, the job has been done. "God has been born," they cried, "we have seen him ourselves. The World is saved. Nothing else matters."
>
> One needn't be much of a psychologist to realise that if this rumour is not stamped out now, in a few years it is capable of diseasing the whole Empire, and one doesn't have to be a prophet to predict the consequences if it should.
>
> (*The Collected Poetry of W. H. Auden* [New York: Random House, 1945], p. 458)

Whether or not the enemies of Christ really believed that he was sent to usher in the rule of God on earth, they were extremely wary of the discomfort that might be produced for them by others who did believe it. They therefore opposed the Christian movement with all the ruthlessness and cunning that were characteristic of men who had not only survived but risen to the top in the hard and unforgiving world of politics. If Jesus himself was not a troublemaker, he was easily seen as the center of a troublesome crowd of people and marked early for public discrediting if not outright elimination. His whole ministry thus became a focus of continual struggle and recrimination, culminating naturally with his death on the cross.

Who was he really, this remarkable man who stood at the center of what was purported to be the arrival of the sovereign reign of God? The interesting thing about the way Matthew describes him (and indeed the other Gospel writers as well) is that he is more important as an *event* than as a person. Almost never is Matthew at pains to show us some intimate detail about the life of Jesus apart from that detail's significance to the rule of God. We do not learn, therefore, whether Jesus was dark or light, had a headful of hair or little at all, liked warm beer, or ate his peas with a knife. We are not even told if he had a wife—as most rabbis did—had any formal schooling, or plied the trade of carpenter. Assuming Matthew knew something about these matters, they were simply not important. The thing that absorbed his attention was the fact—for he believed it to be fact—that God had finally broken the spell of silence and abandonment that lay upon the divine creation by sending the Chosen One to commence the long-promised rule of holiness and righteousness.

What we see in the Gospel, then, is not a carefully focused intimate portrait of Jesus the man, the sort of portrait a reporter for *Time* or *Newsweek* would be interested in obtaining for her readers, but a compelling description of what Jesus did, of the things that happened around him as people came into contact with the rule of God, of the life-and-death struggle enjoined between goodness and evil as his ministry gained in strength and impact. We meet him not as short or tall, educated or uneducated, country or urban, but as preacher, teacher, and healer. The Gospel portrays how he *enacted* the new age that was coming to be.

He was preacher, announcing after the manner of John the Baptist the arrival of the rule of God. He was teacher, following up the announcement with parables, sayings, and interpretations that would enable his disciples to understand how the rule was coming and what they must do to accommodate and serve it. And he was healer, literally and physically touching the lives of countless persons whose faith enabled them to benefit from the interface occurring between the present age and the eternal reign of God. His involvement with the arriving rule was total. It consumed him, came into being through him, eventually caused his death, and then necessitated his Resurrection. His life and ministry were completely inseparable from the coming of the heavenly reign.

This is why, in all the current discussions of the relationship of Christianity to other religions, it is impossible to treat Jesus as merely another leader of unusual insight and illumination. In him, the rule of God has come among us. Not only some high-minded ethical system, as with Confucius. Not only a view of suffering and a way of making the self immune to it, as with Buddha. Not only a sense of discipline and commitment, as with Mahomet. But the rule of God itself.

I will personally go to the mat for the value of several of the non-Christian religions and the importance of our living in dialogue with their adherents. My own existence has been vastly enriched by my readings of the Zen Buddhists, especially D. T. Suzuki, who writes with a clarity and temperament seldom equaled in the modern world. When I lived in Los Angeles and took part in interfaith prayer breakfasts, I often argued with colleagues for the absolute worth of including in our fellowship an individual who was a sort of "bishop" among the thousands of Buddhists in the western states; and I would have been just as keen for the presence of outstanding Hindus or Muslims, had there been such among us.

But as much as I value ecumenical fellowship and understanding, I shall never believe that Christians enter the dialogue among the faiths on a mere parity with others, because Jesus was connected with the actual reign of God. He ushered it in. He preached and taught about it. He performed miracles of healing and restoration within the force field of it. He came back from the grave in the power of it. The early church extended the vision and some of the power of it. Both the vision and the power continue to break out among us. Whereas there is much worth in other religions and it is only the insidiousness of evil in the world that makes enemies of us on the basis of our beliefs, Christianity alone boasts a Master whose very existence is totally bound up with God's establishing of the divine rule within the process of human history.

Within Matthew's Gospel, it is the author's singular focus upon the arrival of divine rule that led him to bring the story of the event of Christ to the first of several climaxes in Simon Peter's confession that Jesus was indeed the Christ (Matt. 16:18). Other climaxes come in chapters 22 through 25, with the parable of the marriage feast, the invectives of Jesus against the scribes and Pharisees, and several other parables about the kingdom of God; chapters 26 and 27, with the betrayal of Jesus and the crucifixion; and chapter 28, with the "great earthquake" (remember Psalm 99:1, where the quaking of the earth was identified with the enthronement of God), the stunning news of the Resurrection, and the commissioning of the eleven faithful disciples. But it is Peter's confession that is the high point of the Gospel, humanly speaking, for it recognizes in brief, summary fashion what the entire story Matthew is telling is about—namely, the arrival of the transcendent realm and Christ's role in it. Once this recognition is achieved, Jesus can be arraigned and put to death, for the knowledge of the divine rule now among us will never die. Its power is *sui generis*; it can continue even without the physical presence of the One who brought it.

Now, given this understanding of the Gospel's hidden structure, that it is entirely about the arrival of the divine rule on earth, we are in a position to place and evaluate the so-called "Beatitudes" at the beginning of chapter 5, and indeed of the entire Sermon on the Mount, which extends through chapter 7, in the overall economy of Matthew's narrative. Jesus' ethical teachings are not *mere* ethical teachings. That is, they are not, like the teachings of Confucius or the maxims of La Rochefoucauld, distillations of moral philosophy intended to direct our paths to an easier or more sociable way of existence. They are instead insights and commandments derivative from the very nature of God's rule, suggestions and directives whose rightness springs from their and our connectedness to the divine reign initiated by Christ himself. As such, they are not mere prescriptions for happier living; they are descriptions of what it means to be a part of the nascent rule of God.

We have been somewhat victimized by centuries of interpretations of the Sermon on the Mount, most of which have begun, in recent years at least, from the premise that Jesus was trying to appeal to our higher selves with a picture of how life ought to be lived, with everyone behaving purely and joyously before God, treating others equitably, and striving to build his or her house on the rock and not on the sand. The truth is that the Sermon on the Mount is not a piece of wonderful advice, a series of thoughts for serene minds set forth with their own inner validity. Their validity springs, on the contrary, from the fact that they are descriptions of life as it is lived within the commonwealth of God, life as it is suddenly viewed when we realize that the enthronement of God long predicted in Hebrew prophecy actually occurred with the coming of Christ.

There has been a lot of discussion over the years about whether the extremely high requirements of the Sermon on the Mount (not hating, not lusting, not swearing by anything, loving one's enemies) are really practicable or were merely intended by Jesus as unreachable standards indicating the perfection of God and the need for humility among human beings. Isolated from the remainder of the Gospel and treated as simple ethical imperatives, the latter would surely be the case; no one can hope to attain to such impossibly rare standards on the basis of human effort and ingenuity alone.

But set the matter within the broader forces of the Gospel, within the entire business of the reign of God and what it means that God has now been enthroned in human history, and the "impossible" standards take on a new complexion. Now they are no longer a set of rules for the uninitiated, a kind of ladder to moral success for anyone who wishes to have a go at it with pluck and determination, but a description of what it is like for us to be caught up in the rule of God and to begin to see life from that perspective instead of the one where we formerly found ourselves. Witness the fact that Matthew has grouped these "impossible" teachings in the format of a sermon delivered to his followers "on the mountain." Luke, on the contrary, cites many of them as being delivered to the people not on the mountain but on a plain. Jesus himself has been to the mountain to pray (Luke 6:12) and to select his disciples (Luke 6:13-16); but then, says Luke:

> He came down with them and stood on a level place, with a great crowd of his disciples and a great multitude of people from all Judea, Jerusalem, and the coast of Tyre and Sidon. They had come to hear him and to be healed of their diseases. . . . Then he looked up at his disciples and said: "Blessed are you who are poor, for yours is the kingdom of God. . . ."   (Luke 6:17-18a, 20)

Matthew, unlike Luke, is intent on identifying Jesus with Moses, the great Hebrew leader who went into the mountain and brought down the law of Yahweh for God's chosen people. Here again God's law is being delivered to the people. Only now God's throne is among the people; the divine rule has been initiated in their midst by the coming of Christ. They are no longer on their own to fulfill the law. The spirit of the living God is within them. They should not only fulfill the law of Moses, they should go beyond it and fulfill the law of Christ. Not only will they not kill, they will not hate; and not only will they not hate, they will actually come to love their enemies. The "impossible" standards are not impossible at all when seen from this vantage point. They are merely descriptive of what it means to live in Christ, as part of the divine rule that has become a living reality in the earth.

I think of the testimony given by a young man named "Danny." Danny had been deeply involved in the drug trade, primarily as an organizer of pushers in major cities. At 22 years of age, he said, he was a millionaire. He owned fast sports cars, a race horse, and a sixty-foot yacht. As a child growing up in a barrio, he had had nothing, not even a pair of shoes or regular meals. Then, within two years of being sent to the United States by the powerful drug interests, he thought he had everything—clothes, cars, girls, all the drugs he wanted, more money than he could spend.

One night a drug-crazed pusher shot Danny three times. For weeks he lay near death in a hospital. No one came to see him, for fear that he had been "marked" by the drug cartel. But one of the orderlies, a young man named Tom, was very kind to him, and when Danny was able to leave the hospital, Tom let him go to his apartment, where he could continue to look after him in the evenings.

Danny could not believe anyone was this kind. But Tom explained that he was a Christian, and that this was the way Christians treated other people. He wouldn't accept anything from Danny for caring for him. Before Danny left Tom's home, he too had become a Christian and had begun to read the Scriptures. When he read about giving up everything for Christ, he thought for two days about whether he could do it. "It will mean going back to the way I was," he said, "without nothing. I wonder if I can do it." He made his decision to do it. "If Christ wants it," he said, "he will help me to do it."

An interviewer asked Danny what he missed most about his life as a rich young drug-peddler. "Do you miss the money?" he asked. "The drugs? The cars?"

Danny could answer the question without taking time to think about it. "None of it," he said. "I don't miss none of it. When Christ comes into your life, I mean really comes into it, he fills you with so much love and excitement that you don't really miss nothing you once thought you'd miss."

I have seen this story repeated with different details dozens of times. A girl who hated her mother until Christ filled her life and she was able to love instead of hate. A businessman in a foreign city on his way to a liaison with a prostitute when he suddenly remembered Christ and was so overcome with emotion that he retraced his steps to his hotel, telephoned his wife, and began a vibrant new life. A woman who was years afterward able to forgive her father, who had raped her repeatedly when she was a teenager. A successful neurologist who turned her back on a prestigious and lucrative practice in an East Coast city to go to Africa as a missionary doctor.

Thomas Chalmers, the great Scottish preacher, had a sermon called "The Expulsive Power of a Great Affection." This is what he meant. When people meet Christ and get swept into the rule of God, their old desires are carried away and they begin to live by a new, higher ethic. It isn't a matter of being told they must behave in a certain manner. It is a matter of a new affection, of having their entire beings reoriented toward God.

Someone else has called it "finding True North in life." Once we have found Christ, our inner compasses are no longer confused about values and priorities. Then we can begin to live like true sons and daughters of the heavenly Father.

There is one more thing, however, to say about the Beatitudes, the beautiful catalog of eight "blessed" sayings at the beginning of the Sermon on the Mount. (The word *beatitude* is from the Latin *beatus,* which means "happy" or "blessed.") Although Jesus may have spoken them at different times, with Matthew gathering them here for esthetic and mnemonic purposes at the start of the sermon, they should not be taken as a list of ethical injunctions of what we are to do to be saved or happy. They are instead statements of fact, observations Jesus made about how the poor in spirit, the mournful, the meek, and so on shall stand in relation to the coming rule of God, which will turn the present structures of existence on their heads and introduce the anti-structures.

Jesus might have expanded these thoughts by saying, "Look around you at all the poverty, grief, humiliation, and hunger for God in the land. In the commonwealth of God, all of this will disappear. The people who are now marginal and afflicted will come into their own, while the wealthy, the proud, and the carefree will suddenly find themselves impoverished and aggrieved."

The parable of the Rich Fool in Luke 12:16-21, whose thoughts were for greater storehouses but was caught up short because he had made no provision for a heavenly treasury, and of the Rich Man and Lazarus in Luke 17:19-31, in which the self-indulgent rich man dies and goes to hell while the poor beggar at his gate dies and is carried into Abraham's bosom, could well be glosses on the Beatitudes. They are not told so much to warn the rich away from their self-destructive behavior patterns as to encourage the poor and the powerless. They say, "There it is, you see, the way the anti-structures will take over and bring compensatory justice to all people, whatever their social status or way of life. You may be burdened and neglected now, but God will straighten everything out when his reign arrives."

It is probably a misuse of the Beatitudes, then, to hold them up as rules for right living, even though they easily lend themselves to that. It would be more to the point to concentrate on Jesus' words later in the Sermon on the Mount, "Strive first for the kingdom of God and his righteousness, and all these things will be given to you as well" (Matt. 6:33). This, after all, is the bottom line of the entire sermon. If the divine rule becomes the foremost thing in our lives, both consciously and unconsciously, then everything else will take care of itself and we shall find ourselves among the blessed ones.

We might call this *pivotal* ethics, in which everything we think and do pivots around a single point, our unyielding and insatiable desire for the approaching commonwealth of God. When we make this the center of all our living, we do not have to worry about mentally ticking off the commandments or the Beatitudes, for we shall automatically and without calculation behave in a manner befitting the children of the Most High. This is why Jesus could respond, when asked about the greatest commandment, by saying, "You shall love the Lord your God with all your heart, and with all your soul, and with all your mind" (Matt. 22:37). And Augustine, who by discovering the rule of God could put behind him a life of libertinism, could say, "Love God and do as you please." When God reigns in our hearts and minds, our ethics will take care of themselves.

Why then, you might ask, should we bother to study the Beatitudes? If they are only descriptive of those who will be rewarded in the commonwealth of God and not prescriptive for those wishing to attain the commonwealth, then surely we should spend our time concentrating on how to center our thoughts on the commonwealth. Ignore the sideshows, get to the big top.

There is merit in that argument.

But why did Jesus bother to formulate the Beatitudes, and Matthew to assemble them thus at the beginning of the Sermon on the Mount? Surely both Jesus and Matthew saw some purpose in their existence. Jesus was not a wordy man. He advised his followers, "Let your word be simply 'Yes, Yes' or 'No, No'" (Matt. 5:37) and "When you are praying, do not heap up empty phrases" (Matt. 6:7). It is highly unlikely that he taught the various "blesseds" unless he had a serious purpose in doing so.

And as for Matthew, it is well known that no scribe was prone to employ mere "filler" in writing something in his day. Papyrus was too scarce and expensive. Our earliest manuscripts of Christian writings reveal that almost no margins were used, and the words were jammed tightly together. Waste was passionately avoided. Matthew didn't arrange the words of Jesus as he did in order to create a flowing, melodic air at the beginning of the Sermon on the Mount. He, too, is bound to have had a serious purpose.

What was this purpose Jesus and Matthew shared? I believe it can be stated in two words: comfort and edification.

It was to encourage all Christ's "little ones" who were still living under the wheel of fortune that was about to turn up for them, and it was to illuminate for others the way of Christ, a way populated with poor, upright, and merciful souls, so that they could find that way attractive and not reprehensible.

How comforting and reassuring the Beatitudes must still be to poor families starving in Ethiopia or Bangladesh, to elderly people taking refuge in sterile apartment houses and mourning for happier times, to young men and women foregoing comfort and prosperity to become missionaries in foreign lands, to public defenders aggrieved at the disparities between rich and poor in the courts of law, to devoted believers adversely treated by an increasingly secular society, to parents in impoverished neighborhoods who wish for a better life for their children, even to those of us who live in reasonable comfort and good standing in our communities but long for peace in the world, honesty in politics, justice in our legal system, and gentleness, kindness, and love in our homes and communities. I have found that even thinking about the Beatitudes as I was writing this book has given a new lift to my spirit. I have been reminded that, while things may appear to be "in the saddle / and ride mankind," as William Wordsworth put it, it will not always be so, because God is already at work in the world bringing about a new regime. No matter how bad things may seem, a new order is on the way. The anti-structures will one day prevail.

There is a beautiful picture of this in Alan Paton's novel *Cry, the Beloved Country*. An old South African pastor, Stephen Kumalo, has gone to Johannesburg to find his son Jonathan. When he finds him, Jonathan is in jail for killing a white lawyer named Arthur Jarvis, who was an advocate of black rights and had written a book about the urgency for justice in that hate-filled country. Kumalo then goes to the elder Jarvis, the lawyer's father, to apologize for his son's crime. Instead of refusing to see him or berating him for Jonathan's deed, Jarvis receives him kindly. He has been reading the manuscript of his son's book, and it has spoken to him of what must be done. Learning that Kumalo's little church in the village of Ndotsheni needs a new house of worship, Jarvis vows to build it for them. He also promises to send great earthmoving equipment and build a dam for the village, so that the people will have a year-round water supply.

The very rumor of what is to be done sends a shock wave of hope through the populace of Ndotsheni. There will be water for irrigation. They can raise cattle. There will be food and milk for the children, so that the young will no longer drift off to the cities to find work. There will be laughter and singing and dancing again. Nothing has happened yet, says Paton; yet it is as if it has. "Although nothing has come yet, something is here already" (New York: Charles Scribner's Sons, 1948, p. 266). Everything is changed.

This is the way it is for the "blessed" ones Jesus describes in the Beatitudes. Nothing has happened yet. They are still poor, tired, and downtrodden. But it is as if everything has changed. The rule of God is on its way.

For those of us not in marginal or deprived situations, all of this should be very instructive. It should help us to see God's "little ones" in a new light. Martin Luther once said, "We need the beggar more than he needs us." That's the point, isn't it? We understand God better when we look at the poor and the innocent and those who strive for peace and realize that God is regarding them favorably. And then, because we too have begun to want the heavenly commonwealth on earth, we begin to imitate the ways of those whom God loves and cares about.

If I see that I shall be judged harshly for living in a nice home and staying warm in winter and cool in summer without caring for the homeless who shiver on the street corner in January and loiter in bus terminals when the temperature is 95 degrees in the shade, I may become more sensitive to the plight of the homeless and work through the many avenues open to a person of my means to effect a better life for them.

If I perceive that God will reward those who "hunger and thirst for righteousness," I may be accused in my own mind for the moral sloth I have permitted myself, saying, "It is not enough to fortify my home and take care of my own family, regardless of what happens to the world out there; I must get involved in the search for more ethical government, fairer laws, and a just society."

If I realize that those with pure hearts actually see God more clearly and wonderfully than I do, then I may begin to seek more disciplined ways of cleansing and renewing my life, so that I, too, may live more sensitively in the presence of the Wholly Other and experience a feeling of the Transcendent permeating even the most mundane aspects of my daily existence.

If I understand that God looks with loving-kindness on those who suffer in some way for their faith, I may start to ponder why it is that I myself am not suffering in any way. Is it because my faith is not strong enough to attract the attention of the powers of evil in the world? Am I merely drifting along, using my religious beliefs as a flotation device in the deep waters, without feeling any concern for the poor souls who flounder beneath me?

What should I be doing that will bring me into conflict with the traditions of the community and the opinions of others?

You see what I mean.

The Beatitudes, prayerfully meditated upon, have the ability to sensitize us to what the rule of God is about and what it really means to walk in the way of Christ. Used by the Spirit of God, they can help us to see the world as God sees it, and thus reorient ourselves to lives of service and humility.

Most of us who have grown up reading and hearing the Beatitudes have probably lost our sense of their true radicality, of the way they reflect not the structures of our world but the anti-structures. The world says that rich is happy; the Beatitudes say that poor in spirit is. The world says that gaiety and the partying spirit is happy; the Beatitudes say that mourning is. The world says that machoism and invulnerability are happy; the Beatitudes say that meekness is. The world says that learning to live cleverly in the midst of sleaze is happy; the Beatitudes say that hungering and thirsting for righteousness is. The world says that tough-mindedness and obduracy is happy; the Beatitudes say that mercy is. The world says that perversion and addiction and underhandedness is happy; the Beatitudes say that purity of heart is. The world says that being adept at conflict is happy; the Beatitudes say that the spirit of peacemaking is. The world says that staying on everybody's good side and not making waves is happy; the Beatitudes say that coming under fire for Christ's sake is.

Anti-structures.

Not the way the world is, but the way God is going to make it.

And, in the meantime, being apprised of how things are going to be, completely without our help and solely by the will of God, may help us to tune into how we ought to live and what is best for us personally.

There is a picture of how it works in Joseph F. Girzone's *Joshua*, a novel about Jesus as a contemporary wood artist with the Hebrew name of Joshua. Joshua has moved into a small house on the edge of a fictional town called Auburn. He lives very simply, very openly, and with kindness and generosity toward everyone. Suspicious at first because he is a stranger with ways unlike their own, the townspeople eventually come to like and admire him.

One day a Jewish factory owner, Aaron Fahn, speaks to him about the way he is, and wants to know how he came to be that way. Joshua wants to know why he asks.

"Because I can't understand how anyone could develop the vision of life that you have. It is so foreign to my way of thinking, and so different from the thinking of everybody I know."

"Each person," says Joshua, "looks at life through a different vision. Three men can look at a tree. One man will see so many board feet of valuable lumber worth so much money. The second man will see it as so much firewood to be burned, to keep his family warm in the winter. The third man will see it as a masterpiece of God's creative art, given to man as an expression of God's love and enduring strength, with a value far beyond its worth in money or firewood. What we live for determines what we see in life and gives clear focus to our inner vision."

Aaron asks, "Who taught you to think that way?"

"It is what I see," says Joshua. "You could see it, too, if you could detach yourself from the things you were taught to value. They do not give you peace, nor do they give you lasting satisfaction. They leave you empty, and filled with a longing for something more."

Aaron admits that is true, but wants to know how Joshua knows it.

"I know how man was made," says Joshua, "and understand what he really needs if he is to grow and find peace" (New York: Macmillan Co., 1987, p. 67).

This is why the Beatitudes are important, and why Matthew places them at the beginning of Jesus' great sermon. They are a statement of how we are really made, in God's spiritual design for things, and how happiness really comes to us. And even if they are spoken apocalyptically, as the way it will be when the true structures of God have overtaken the present structures of the world, they can become wonderful guides to finding a life of joy and fulfillment.

CHAPTER ONE

BLESSED ARE THE POOR IN SPIRIT

Blessed are the poor in spirit, for theirs is the kingdom of heaven" (Matt. 5:3).

We are in interpretive trouble at the very outset of the beatitudes. What did Jesus mean by "the poor in spirit"? Was he talking about the truly poor, people who begged for food and had no home to sleep in and no one to care for them? Or was he referring to an attitude of lowliness and humility, the poverty of the spirit cultivated by certain monks in the Middle Ages?

The Greek word for "poor" is *ptochos.*

It is an ugly word. Pronounced *puh-TOH-kohs.*

Say it.

Puh-TOH-kohs.

It means "desperately poor."

It speaks of a poverty so deep, so chronic, that it is actually hopeless.

Most of us who can read a book or hold a library card or even visit a bookstore occasionally do not really comprehend this kind of poverty. We watch the TV pictures of half-naked bodies squatting in the dust of some African village, hands reaching up in cuplike fashion, eyes searching blankly, asking for help but expecting nothing; and we have no way, as we sit on our cushioned sofas munching snackfood and drinking diet colas, of even beginning to understand the simple life-or-death plight of such people.

They belong to the *ptochos.*

We get off the interstate on the way through the South to visit Disney World, pausing only for fuel and to use the bathroom on the edge of some all-but-dead little town called Carter's Cove or Twin Oaks or Pippa Passes, not even noticing where we are, and maybe we see for a moment, obliquely and with our peripheral vision only, a few children, their noses running, standing listlessly in the weeds and dirt beside the station, or a couple of men in overalls, their faces prematurely creased and slack at the same time, sitting on a makeshift bench outside the room with the greaserack, talking in low voices if they speak at all, and there is no way we can enter into the sparse, shadowy world where they exist, where bookstores and concert halls and even movie houses are unknown and the homes are shanties with bare light bulbs hanging from the ceilings and there is no indoor plumbing and the food on the table is usually scarce, bland, and starchy.

They too belong to the *ptochos.*

We walk the streets of the inner city trying not to look at the ragged beggars growing more numerous these days, their clothes often too thin in winter and too thick in summer, unkempt and unshaven because they have no bathroom for cleaning themselves up, not even on an occasional basis, their skin swarthy and dark-complexioned from spending so much time in the streets and alleys, soaking up diesel fumes from the trucks and buses constantly roaring away from the curb, their clothes filthy and smelly from never being washed, their shoes tattered and worn from walking and standing always on hard surfaces, their eyes fixed and hopeless from inadequate diet and undoctored illnesses and drinking hair tonic or cheap wine to forget their troubles, and we cannot possibly imagine what it is like to exist that way, perduring mindlessly through the seasons and waiting only to die, not to live.

They also are part of the *ptochos.*

And they are of course only a small part. Most of the *ptochos* live in underdeveloped nations, the so-called Third World. Like the poor of our own country, the Third World poor are the victims of economic forces beyond their control. They didn't choose to be poor. And their poverty is not merely a result of their ignorance and illiteracy. In many instances, it is a result of something people in other nations did. The Europeans developed military superiority and used it to subdue the peoples of Africa, the Near East, Central and South America. Then they colonized these parts of the globe and used them to supply the raw materials needed for the Industrial Revolution. Instead of investing their profits in the peoples of these areas, they used them to become rich in their own nations, thus creating an even greater disparity between them and the native populations. This left the despoiled areas subject to predators, diseases, and the ravages of nature, such as earthquakes, droughts, and floods. Millions of the world's poor now live along the edges of the Sahara, which steadily advances against land that was once used for farming and grazing, or in such unmanageable areas as the floodplain of Bangladesh. They have nowhere else to go.

I heard Bob Seiple, president of World Vision, International, telling about a woman he had seen in Adjubar, Ethiopia. She had walked two days to receive a monthly allowance of grain distributed by the great hunger organization, and would walk two days carrying it home. She had barely received it when she set it down to rest for a moment and someone stole it. She returned to the food line in tears. The tears were not for herself but for her child, the only surviving child of eight she had borne. The other seven had died in the famine of 1983–1985, and her husband, weakened from hunger, had died of disease.

The desperately poor.

So poor that they don't expect things ever to get any better for them.

Resigned.

Given up.

Hopeless.

But Jesus said they will be happy in the kingdom. In fact, he said, they are the ones to whom the kingdom belongs.

A scandalous thought, which may be why Matthew's text of Jesus' words reads "the poor in spirit."

Luke's doesn't. He has Jesus saying, "Blessed are you who are poor, for yours is the kingdom of God" (Luke 6:20).

Some scholars believe this was the earlier reading, the real words of Jesus, and that some well-meaning editor in the first century after the Gospels were compiled, thinking the original saying too harsh for persons even as well-off as himself, softened it enormously by adding the words "in spirit." Blessed are the poor *in spirit*. A radically different thing. The loop widened to include more well-to-do Christians whose hearts were in the right place, who loved the poor and contributed to their welfare and generally used the world's goods to prepare the way for the preaching of the kingdom.

An attorney friend of mine who is not exactly poor in the world's-goods department argues that Jesus probably did say "the poor in spirit," because, he says, there is no one who is poorer than one whose spirit is impoverished, who no longer has a heart for living. "That is real poverty," he maintains.

And such a possibility is not far from a word spoken by a minister in a conference I was leading. We were talking about this text and wondering whether Jesus meant simply the poor or, on the other hand, the low in spirit. Then a pastor who had worked for years in an inner-city environment spoke up and said that for him the phrase had long seemed applicable to a lot of the people he met who were so poor, and had been poor for so very long, that they had lost all hope of ever being anything but poor.

"That is different from the kind of poverty some of us experience," he said. "When I was a seminary student serving a small rural church, my wife and I never had enough money to pay our car payment, our insurance bill, and some leftover medical expenses in the same month. We were always doing a balancing act just to stay a step ahead of the bill collectors. Looking back on it now, I realize we were poor. But it didn't bother us much, because we knew it was only temporary. We didn't expect to become rich, but we believed we would one day own our own home and have money to meet normal obligations.

"But the people I met in the inner city," he continued, "seldom had such hope. Most of them were poorer than they had been at some earlier time, had been that way for years, and finally lost hope that things would ever get any better for them.

"That," he concluded, "is 'poor in spirit.'"

Personally, I find this explanation persuasive, because it reconciles Matthew's report on the words of Jesus with the harder reading in Luke's Gospel, preserving the emphasis on the desperate poverty of the people Jesus was talking about. As I said in the introduction, Jesus' teachings were radical and revolutionary, standing our usual conceptions of things on their heads, and it ill behooves us to try to adjust them to suit our own circumstances. Jesus probably did mean that the Kingdom will be given to the despicably poor of the earth, those who have fallen through the cracks of the social system and are held in greatest disdain by the rich and powerful persons of the society.

Such a viewpoint is after all consistent with numerous other references to Jesus' teachings about poverty and wealth. When he told the parable of the sower, he described the seed sown among the thorns as being the way it is with the gospel when it is heard by anyone in whom "the cares of the world and the delight in riches" grow up and choke out the tender plant (Matt. 13:22; Mark 4:19; Luke 8:14).

When he met the rich ruler who was such an attractive man and had kept the commandments scrupulously all his life, Jesus said he lacked one thing, and told him to sell everything he had, give to the poor, and come, follow him (Matt. 19:21; Luke 18:22). When the man could not bring himself to part with his riches, Jesus said, "How hard, it is for those who have wealth to enter the kingdom of God! Indeed, it is easier for a camel to go through the eye of a needle than for someone who is rich to enter the kingdom of God" (Luke 18:24-25).

Another time, Jesus told the parable of the rich man whose lands produced so plentifully that he planned to pull down his inadequate barns and build greater ones. In the end, though, he died without getting to enjoy his great wealth and God called him a fool. "So it is," said Jesus, "with those who store up treasures for themselves but are not rich toward God" (Luke 12:21).

And there is the parable of the rich man and Lazarus, about a man so wealthy that he lived in purple, the clothing of royalty, and dined sumptuously every day while a poor, diseased man lay at his gate wishing only for what fell from the rich man's table. When they died, the poor man was carried by the angels to Abraham's bosom—the kingdom of heaven?—and the rich man found himself in the torments of Hades (Luke 16:19-31).

All of which spells trouble for us—for me, a man writing this book on a word processor surrounded by books and paintings and mementos, and for you, a person able to buy a book or visit a library. The very fact that we have a *door*, a convenience for locking up our possessions and shutting out the world, puts us in danger of being like the rich man with a gate. Like him, we have a place where the poor can lie. Some of us are even better off than he was, and keep a wider median between us and the ultra-poor. We live in attractive neighborhoods where the poor aren't allowed. If a shabbily dressed person shows up in the vicinity, someone in the Neighborhood Watch calls the police and they cruise around to keep an eye on the person. Being successful means that we don't have to live in the ghettos or crumbling areas where suffering is most evident. It distances us from the *ptochos,* the desperately poor, and defines us as the not-poor, at least by Jesus' standards.

Of course it all depends on your way of thinking.

We are usually raised to believe that having things is a sign of success and a form of blessedness. This is natural in an acquisitive society. Education is sold to the public for its utilitarian purposes. "You'll never have a good job if you don't graduate from high school." "You won't have a chance at the best jobs if you don't go to college." Good jobs, big money, houses in the suburbs, expensive cars, membership in the country club, easy credit, positions of respect. Our whole society is convinced of the value of these things and reendorses them in each succeeding generation.

Maybe it all began modestly, with the Puritan teachings about thrift and hard work. God honors discipline and industry, they said.

Now it is all-consuming.

I tried a little experiment with the television set. Using the remote-control switch, I turned it on four times at random during a late afternoon and evening, and, starting with the channel at one end of the band, ran through all the channels until I reached the other end. It was a simple exercise to see how many times I ran into an advertisement instead of a program.

There are thirty channels on our set, including two public channels, a weather channel, an all-sports channel, and two continuous news channels.

The first time, I hit fifteen ads.

The second time, fourteen.

The third time, seventeen.

The fourth time, twenty-two.

What does this say about our society? It literally depends on people's acquiring things. We are no longer a simple farming society, where people raise their own food and treat manufactured items as luxuries. We are a society of makers and sellers and consumers, where everything depends on hype and sales, and people listen daily for the news from the marketplace to see how healthy we are as a nation.

Designers of shopping malls make them larger and larger, billing each one as the most modern, the most elegant, and the most convenient ever built.

Banks compete with one another for architectural dash and grandiosity.

Car dealerships all try to be the snazziest and largest in the area.

Churches vie with one another to have the biggest sanctuary, the most expansive parking lot, the softest pews, the loveliest windows, the tallest spire.

It all spells *Rich, Rich, Rich.*

And unfortunately for all of us this idea of richness is what we are exporting to the underdeveloped nations of the world. Western-made movies are shown daily in every major Third World city, and our television shows are a primary source of programming in almost every country outside of continental Europe, Great Britain, and Japan. People in Pakistan, Guatemala, the Philippines, Zambia, and Peru watch "Dallas," "Falcon Crest," "Wheel of Fortune," and "The Price Is Right." Then they want the American life-style, complete with Western clothes, fancy cars, big houses, and lots of charge cards.

Rich, Rich, Rich.

More than two decades ago, John Updike published his stunning novel *Rabbit, Run.* Its protagonist—one could hardly call him a hero—was Harry Angstrom, a young man who had been a basketball star in high school and now, as a nervous young seller of potato peelers, couldn't settle down and was always on the run.

In the subsequent volume, *Rabbit Redux,* Harry was older and had more responsibilities, but still couldn't settle down. He cheated on his wife and left home when his son Nelson was a boy, unable to face up to the tasks of fatherhood.

Then came two more volumes, *Rabbit Is Rich* and *Rabbit at Rest. Rabbit at Rest* is the end of the tetralogy, and there is a pun in the word *rest*. It refers to Harry's death, which is the only way he finally finds rest from the strains and worries of mortal existence.

What does it mean, in the third volume, for Rabbit (or Harry) to be rich? In his forties, he has inherited, with his wife, one-half of his father-in-law's company, Springer Motors, one of two Toyota dealerships in the Brewer area. The other half belongs to his wife's mother, Bessie Springer. Harry and his wife Janice live in Bessie Springer's house, and his life is bounced around among three locations—the house, the showroom of the dealership, and the Brewer country club, where he regularly plays golf with three buddies and drinks with them and their wives. Finally, after Harry and Janice's son Nelson comes home from college and marries Pru—a girl he has gotten pregnant—and Nelson and Pru have moved into the Springer home too, he and Janice put $15,600 down on a little stone house in the suburbs that costs $78,000 and escape to their idea of the good life and the American dream.

Harry despises himself, fights with his son, goes to bed with a friend's wife, has a big gut from drinking too much, feels depressed most of the time because there is no meaning in his existence, and manages, with his mother-in-law, a car dealership in a world where gas supplies are dwindling and cars will soon be a thing of the past.

This is rich?

That is the irony in the title, of course, and in the American dream itself. Harry Angstrom, in this volume, has become George Babbitt, the stout, all-American citizen of Sinclair Lewis's satire. He has risen from poverty to become a leading citizen in his community. He owns property. He plays the market in gold and silver. He commands a work force. He takes vacations in the Poconos and the Bahamas. He is rich, by the world's standards.

But not by Christ's, who said "Blessed are the poor in spirit, for theirs is the kingdom of heaven."

People get confused, said Jesus, when it comes to happiness. They think being rich leads to feeling good. It doesn't.

When you are rich, you have to worry about everything—your business, your house, your jewels and silverware, your investments, insurance, security, people who work for you, people always wanting something from you, your reputation, your appearance, everything. Somehow it all gets between you and God, like a cloud that drifts between you and the sun.

Real happiness—*blessedness*—is being poor and realizing that God owns the world. Then the cloud isn't there.

Maybe the problem with being rich, with owning anything, is the one Gabriel Marcel, the French philosopher, recognized years ago in his book *Being and Having*. There is a sense, said Marcel, in which the tables always get turned and anything we think we possess really exercises possession over us. The big house a woman has always wanted turns her into a slave to take care of it. The high office to which a man has always aspired demands all his time and energy to maintain it. Thus owning anything means being owned, and having property diminishes our sense of inner being.

If we would be free—especially free to enjoy God—then we have to relinquish our sense of ownership.

So Jesus told the rich ruler to sell everything and give the proceeds to the poor.

And one of the great rules of the monastic system became the rule of poverty.

And Tolstoy, the Russian novelist, gave away all his possessions, even after he was rich and famous.

And Mother Teresa spent her Nobel Prize money opening another center for the wretchedly poor.

And Kagawa, the great Japanese saint, wrote these words about finding God:

> God dwells among the lowliest of men. He sits on the dust-heap among the prison convicts. With the juvenile delinquents He stands at the door, begging bread. He throngs with the beggars at the place of alms. He is among the sick. He stands in line with the unemployed in front of the free employment bureaus.
>
> Therefore, let him who would meet God visit the prison cell before going to the temple. Before he goes to church let him visit the hospital. Before he reads his Bible let him help the beggar standing at his door. (Toyohiko Kagawa, "Meditations," cited in William Axling, *Kagawa* [London: SCM Press, 1946], p. 38)

How Jesus' vision of this new world, the Kingdom, judges us! I remember when I was the pastor of a large, wealthy church in the West, and how some of the members reacted to the street people who came to our doors.

I remember the usher, dressed in a morning coat and striped pants, who saw a poor, bearded man approach the coffee table where some sweets had been placed, grabbed up the silver tray holding the cakes and cookies and whisked them away to safety, berating over his shoulder, "These are not for *you*!"

I remember the lady who managed the church's thrift shop, and how she responded when a concerned church member said that the prices in the shop were too high. "We set them that way," she said, "to keep out the riffraff."

And I remember the Easter Day when several street folks, scruffy and poorly dressed, came up to me in my white robes in the forecourt after the last service and asked if it was all right for them to enter the church. I directed them inside and returned to greet the people remaining in the forecourt. When I didn't see them emerge from the church after a few minutes, I stepped inside to check on them, and saw them standing around in the huge sanctuary. With the suspicious nature born of having things, I suggested to a custodian that he keep an eye on them, and I went back outside.

When all the members and visitors had departed, I stepped back into the sanctuary. At first I didn't see the street people. I walked down the aisle. There they were, all of them, scattered across the front of the chancel, kneeling in prayer.

I stood there breathless for a moment, watching them. Tears formed in my eyes. I had never seen anything so beautiful. When at last they began to look up, I walked among them and asked if they would like me, as the pastor, to offer a prayer for us all. They said yes, and I knelt among them, shepherd of a new flock, my hands on the shoulders of two of them, and prayed the most heartfelt prayer I had prayed that day.

Theirs is the kingdom of heaven.

What hope is there for the rest of us?

Jesus told the rich ruler, "Go, sell your possessions, and give the money to the poor" (Matt. 19:21).

Help with the leveling.

Work to make things better.

Promote sharing and healing.

The implication was that it would complete the spirituality of the ruler. Then he would be all right in God's eyes.

Maybe we can do the same.

In Abingdon, England, in the Church of St. Nicholas, there is a colorful plaque honoring the memory of John Blacknall and his wife, citizens of Abingdon, who died together, probably of plague, in the year 1625. Apparently they gave everything they had to the church to establish an endowment for the town's poor, and even today, almost four centuries later, it is used to set fresh bread daily on the altar, where the poor can come to eat and worship.

Think how many souls, when God's kingdom has fully come and the anti-structures are in place, will rise up to bless the names of John Blacknall and his wife.

I think they did what the rich ruler was supposed to do but couldn't.

CHAPTER TWO

BLESSED
ARE THOSE WHO
MOURN

Blessed are those who mourn, for they will be comforted"
(Matt. 5:4).

Ah, now, there is something we can relate to! We may not be poor, but most of us know a bit about mourning.

We have lost parents and children and siblings and friends.

And more besides.

We have lost homes and jobs and illusions and contests and hopes and dreams.

Judith Viorst, whose *Necessary Losses* is already a classic in our time, says:

> When we think of loss we think of the loss, through death, of people we love. But loss is a far more encompassing theme in our life. For we lose not only through death, but also by leaving and being left, by changing and letting go and moving on. And our losses include not only our separations and departures from those we love, but our conscious and unconscious losses of romantic dreams, impossible expectations, illusions of freedom and power, illusions of safety—and the loss of our own younger self, the self that thought it always would be unwrinkled and invulnerable and immortal. (New York: Ballantine Books, 1987, p. 2)

Viorst's book is about the inevitability of such losses in all our lives, and how we actually grow by learning to deal with them. She is of course right. We are not stones, that have no linear stories to tell, but living organisms. Change occurs in our lives all the time, whether we are willing to face it or not. So we might as

41

well learn to recognize it and turn it to whatever advantage we can.

But oh, it is so hard, isn't it?

I remember a six-year period in my life when everything seemed to change.

First, I left a wonderful job I had had for fifteen years and moved to another state. We had to part with the home we had built—the most comfortable, uniquely designed house we ever had, set on the loveliest lot in the most convenient location. We often called it our Shangri-La. Our children had grown up there, so we left behind the physical setting of hundreds of significant memories, including their beautiful school only a block away. I left a capacious office where I had read many books, written thousands of letters, and met with countless students and colleagues. We left the familiar stores where we had shopped for years, the streets we had walked and driven, the churches we had worshiped in, the friends with whom we had loved and argued and laughed over the years. I thought my heart would break. My family felt the same way. One of our sons cried all the way to our new home. When our furniture had been picked up and the house was empty, my wife and I walked through it, grieving for every room we were leaving. She put her arms around a support beam in the carport and wept and wept. I literally had to pry her loose to get her into the car.

Two years later, my mother died. It was not completely unexpected. She had been a smoker and had terrible emphysema. My wife has often said she wishes we had video taped Mama's last years of life and could show the tape to everyone who insists on smoking. But when my father called and told me she had died, it was nevertheless a surprise. We lived a full day's journey by car, and it was almost impossible to fly. The funeral was in Mama's church. I gave the main prayer over her body, and wept as I did it. Something had happened. There was an immense hole in the fabric of my existence. The woman who had given me birth, who had loved me unconditionally all my life, was gone.

It was not all bad. I had a wonderful dream the night after she died. In the dream, my wife Anne and I were at a tropical seaport, seeing Mama off on a journey. A great ocean-going vessel was docked beside us. There were palm trees swaying in the wind. The crowd was happy and spirited. Mama looked younger than she had for years. She was the way she had been when she was middle aged, and she was dressed beautifully for the trip. There was a woman with her, a traveling companion who was to look after her on the journey. We said happy good-byes and they went aboard. Anne and I stood there waving to them as the ship pulled out, bound for ports unknown.

But I still felt the loss when I awakened the next morning.

Shortly after this, our younger son, who was the first to leave home, went off to college. We were thoughtful about that for several weeks, and shed some tears when we deposited him on the campus and bade him good-bye. Two or three years later, our other son, who had lived at home while attending college, left to go to graduate school. Then, a year later, he married and we thought he had gone away for good. My wife and I held hands and looked at each other across the dinner table. Was this the way all those happy years of child raising had to end? I didn't think I could stand it.

The following year, my father died. He had become ill almost immediately after Mother's death. They had argued a lot when she was alive—or *he* had argued a lot, for she was a more passive, introverted person—but he had been intimately attached to her, especially in the last decade of their lives. We talked about having him come to live with us, but that didn't prove workable on either side. Once, we had it arranged for him to move into a home only fifty miles from us, where I could have visited him at least once a week. But in the end he chose to remain in the little town in Kentucky where he had lived for the last forty-three years. He didn't like changes. So we drove down to see him as often as we could, which, in the last year, when he was often in the hospital, was about every other month. I watched him slip away. He lost weight steadily. His powers of memory evaporated. His now thin body stood erect, a gaunt reminder of the powerful man he had been when he was young and could pitch hay into a hayloft faster than any of the men who worked with him.

I conducted Dad's funeral myself. He hadn't been to church for anything but a wedding or a funeral in fifty years. A friend told me he said he had once been hurt in the church and didn't go back. It didn't seem right to have the service in a sanctuary, so we did it under the tent at the gravesite.

A funny thing happened while it was going on. It was a beautiful spring morning when we began. The sun was shining brightly and the birds were chirping in the nearby trees. Suddenly, as I was having the prayer, a frigid wind descended, the sky became dark, we were pelted by hail, the tent flaps whipped noisily, the flowers blew over, and everyone present felt as if some great, demonic power were struggling for possession of my father's soul. My wife said afterward that I had to shout to make my words heard, though I was standing only two or three feet from the little band of mourners. But, as suddenly as the day had changed, it changed again, and when the prayer was finished the sun was shining, the birds were singing as before, and what had occurred seemed to have happened in a dream.

Speaking of dreams, I had a wonderful dream about my father, too, just as I had dreamed about my mother. The night after his death, I dreamed that I saw Mother coming down the hill in a meadow filled with flowers. She was young and barefoot, and dressed in a beautiful peasant dress. Then I saw my father walking up the hill toward her. He, too, was barefoot, with his trousers rolled partway up to his knees. And he was young, as she was. She reached out her hand toward him, and he took it and they went up the hill together, as fresh and beautiful and innocent as they had been when they were courting more than fifty years before.

We buried Dad in April. In August we sold our home in Virginia, where I had been a pastor for six years, said good-bye to our children and hosts of friends, and moved all the way across the country to California. Now we were separated by 2,500 miles from our territorial nexus as well as our friends and family. And, to top it all, the moving company employed some careless men who allowed a lot of our furniture to get damaged and about one-third of my library to become water-soaked and ruined. I remember standing in our garage one afternoon, going through box after box of books, wiping off the volumes that could be salvaged, and at one point simply weeping at the sense of desolation that flooded over me.

I am not sure I have ever fully recovered from the feelings of grief that assailed me during those years. I probably go for weeks at a time without thinking directly of my parents or the homes we left or the friends we've had to say good-bye to. But there is something in me that has known loss and known it so deeply that it will never forget. There is a sense of evanescence and impermanence that haunts the underside of my consciousness. Some mornings I wake up having dreamed of my parents or of my children's growing-up years and there is a taste of sadness in my mouth. Only the night before last I had a vivid dream about my dad. He was young and strong, as he had been when he was about forty. I touched his arm and thought it felt like an anvil. I put my arms around him and told him I loved him. But then I woke up and realized he was not there, it was only a dream. I began the day by thinking about the way we touch and let go in life, touch and let go.

William Barclay says in *The Plain Man Looks at the Beatitudes* that the Greek word *penthein*, which is translated "to mourn" in the Gospels, "is one of the strongest words for mourning in the Greek language," and that it generally signifies sorrow for the dead. (London: Fontana Books, 1963, p. 25) Perhaps it does. But the general associations for mourning in the Bible suggest that death plays only a small part in human grieving and that our hearts can be heavy about much besides the passing of a loved one. In the prophetic literature, especially Isaiah and Jeremiah, the most frequent use of the Hebrew verb *abal*, translated "to mourn," is with the noun "earth."

"The earth mourns and withers," says Isaiah, "the world languishes and withers" (Isa. 24:4 RSV). "The land mourns and languishes; Lebanon is confounded and withers away; Sharon is like a desert" (Isa. 33:9).

"Because of this the earth shall mourn," says Jeremiah, "and the heavens above grow black" (Jer. 4:28). "How long will the land mourn, and the grass of every field wither?" (Jer. 12:4) "Judah mourns and her gates languish; they lie in gloom on the ground, and the cry of Jerusalem goes up" (Jer. 14:2).

Such images are usually connected to the desolation brought upon the earth by human sin. The inhabitants of the earth mourn because life is fragile and uncertain, because God sends plagues and floods and fire upon the people, because life is simply hard to bear in this mortal frame. Mourning is the opposite of joy and laughter (see Matt. 9:14-15; Luke 6:25). It is the sadness that accompanies the recognition of our mortality, of our powerlessness before the onslaughts of time and decay, of the inevitability that everything now living will die.

A few years ago I was in Japan, conducting seminars for U.S. military chaplains. One day we were having a sharing session in which we talked about the most intimate things on our minds. One young chaplain had just returned from his mother's funeral in the States. He told us about his father, who had always been a strong, take-charge sort of man, and how he had collapsed into helplessness over the mother's death. The night after the funeral, the father went to bed and the chaplain sat in the living room, writing some notes. There was a shuffling noise in the hall, and the father stood in the doorway, looking scared and pitiful. "Son," he said, "I can't go to bed by myself. I have slept with your mother for forty years, and I can't bear to be by myself. Will you come and sleep with me tonight?"

The chaplain did. He dressed for bed and got in beside his father. The father curled up in a fetal position and backed up against his son, and the son held him like a baby through the night.

The chaplain's eyes were red with tears as he told us this. "Life is so wonderful," he said, "and so hard to bear."

So wonderful and so hard to bear.

That is what mourning is about.

It is about our sense of finiteness, of the way everything will pass.

It can attack us when we are staring at our children, or watching the leaves turn brown in the fall, or sitting by a loved one in the hospital, or noticing how a neighborhood has run down, or realizing we are developing arthritis in our joints, or observing that the roses in a vase on the table have wilted since yesterday. It can creep over us when we look through an old picture album, or stand behind an elderly person in the checkout line at the grocery store, or find that our eyesight is getting worse for reading the telephone book, or see that the house needs painting again, or watch a familiar landmark being torn down to make way for something else, or hear that someone we knew has died.

Somewhere in my journals there is an entry about how strongly it hit me one day as I was sitting in the chancel of a church, waiting to deliver the guest sermon. A beautiful woman was playing a violin solo. Her lovely hands worked continuously at the frets and the bow, evoking the most soulful music I thought I had ever heard. There was a rose pinned in her exquisitely coiffed hair. I was transported. Then a dark thought crossed my mind, as if it had been a cloud passing between me and the sun. In a few years, the woman would become old. The rose in her hair would die. Her soft hands would be gnarled and wrinkled by age. She would stop playing the instrument. She would be confined to a bed or a wheelchair. Then she, too, would die.

The music brought me back again to a realization of how beautiful it was. But I did not recover from the image of the violinist as an old woman. It haunted me for days.

Mourning is about death and change and loss and deterioration and weakness and sadness and everything else that bespeaks our limitations and humanity, our temporalness and expendability. Once it has come upon us, it is very hard to dispel. It afflicts us when we least expect it, and mocks us in every hour of triumph.

The very fact that Jesus said "Blessed are those who mourn" must of course mean that there are people who do not mourn, or who are seldom afflicted by the sense of mutability and decay that disturbs the rest of us.

Who did Jesus have in mind?

Were these the Pharisees, the ultra-righteous people of the Gospels who seemed so self-congratulatory over the uprightness of their existence? Perhaps there is a kind of immunity to sadness and despair in people who think very highly of themselves, a refusal to be bothered by the thoughts of mortality and futility that beseige others.

I have known a few such persons, I think. Vain, ego-centered and self-serving. Always thinking of what would please them, and never of the feelings or needs or desires of others. Always brooding over their own images and heedless of the wounds they caused in others' psyches. Down deep, as one movie actress put it, they are really very shallow. Bent invariably on their own goals and pleasures, they seem not to notice the sad estate of so many in the world, or the fact that life, like a highway, is strewn with the wrecks of other lives spent in the pursuit of fame, fun, and fortune.

Charles Dickens's Scrooge was such a character, I think, until his encounter with Marley's ghost and the specters of the three Christmases. He had no sympathy for the man who worked for him or the man's poor family, and when accosted by men soliciting funds for those in the poorhouses, he scoffed at the very idea of charity, suggesting that there were prisons built for those who could not pay their debts. He seemed incapable of reflection on the past and moved instead relentlessly on toward the future, living with a kind of rigorous self-discipline he expected of others, as well as himself. Only when the three Christmas spirits forced him to review his own childhood and adolescence, and to revisit the young woman to whom he was once engaged, was the fire of humanity rekindled in his cold heart, returning him to love, joy, and generosity.

Who are the Scrooges of our time, the people determined to make a profit while those around them mourn the tragedies of life and the misfortunes of the poor? Are they the Wall Street brokers who drive relentlessly forward in the acquisition of personal fortunes—including yachts and cars and plush apartments—at the expense of thousands of small investors? The elite surgeons and internists who are too busy cramming their appointment schedules and collecting fees to care about the fears and apprehensions of the patients herded like cattle through their offices? The legal experts who gouge, contest, and wrangle for 40 percent of their clients' awards and then anesthetize their sensibilities in country clubs and suburban splendor? Maybe even the ministers whose unbridled ambitions have carried them to prestigious churches where they don't have to cope with the homeless and hungry of the world?

I hope none of these is so insulated against caring and feeling that he or she is never moved to tears by the human condition—by the sight of an old man fishing in a worn purse for money to pay for a bus ride or the picture of a woman of indeterminate age searching through a trash can at the edge of the sidewalk for bottles and rags to sell or the image of a small child chasing gleefully after soap bubbles released to float and dip in the currents of air, only to cut his feet on the broken bottles that sparkle like fallen stars on the compacted earth of the inner-city lot. I am by nature an optimist and always believe that there is—beneath the coldest, gruffest exterior in a person I know—a place of tenderness and feeling if only it can be discovered and excavated. Yet I recognize that there are people capable of the stoniest, most impenetrable attitudes, who can pull wings off butterflies and cripple dogs in the street and mug or rape human victims without either sympathy or remorse. The hideous crimes of some of the Nazi camp commanders and of certain jailers and inquisitors in more recent prisons and of crazy killers like Charles Manson and of Lieutenant William Calley, Jr. who annihilated all those civilians at My Lai in Vietnam suggest a callousness and remoteness from the common suffering that boggle the mind. Yet they exist, they are there, and they are chronicled in the daily papers and news reports of every nation on earth.

Some would say that cynics do not mourn, that they are coldly aloof in a world of hurt feelings and broken dreams. But it has been my experience that most cynics are people capable of great sentiment who have managed, across the years, to protect themselves by developing a cynical, critical attitude toward everything around them. Deeply wounded at some time in their lives—perhaps by a cruel parent or a thoughtless teacher or a quarrelsome spouse—they have learned to encase their sensibilities in a prickly, apparently unsentimental view of the world and even become evangelists of cynicism to the people around them who appear to accept almost everything without examination. One of the favorite stereotypes of the movies is the crusty old fellow who never admits to normal human feelings until something happens in the plot to expose the gentle, tenderhearted person down under the façade.

The truth is that almost everybody mourns at some time or other in his or her life, whether for a lost childhood or a kind friend who moved away or a parent who died or a way of life that is gone. A friend of mine who is a chaplain in a state penitentiary system says that he has yet to meet a criminal so hardened that there is not someone or something he or she misses, however cleverly the person manages to conceal it from others. The sense of grief, as far as we can tell, is universal. It may be more extensive and apparent in some than in others, but it is a part of all human experience.

What then was Jesus saying in this beatitude?

Maybe he was not so much trying to isolate a class of people—namely, the mourners—as to describe the kingdom, the coming anti-structures, in which all pain and grief would be banished forever. This would certainly agree with John's vision of the new heaven and new earth in the book of Revelation, in which he said God would be in the midst of the saints and would "wipe every tear from their eyes. Death will be no more; mourning and crying and pain will be no more" (Rev. 21:4).

It would also agree with the occasions when Jesus returned people from the dead, reuniting them with loved ones who had been grieving for them. Think of the wonderful story in Luke 7:11-17, of the time when Jesus and his disciples were entering the little town of Nain and met a funeral procession coming toward them. A young man had died, and his widowed mother was among the mourners. Jesus and his friends probably heard the clamor at a great distance, because it was customary in those days not only for the family of the departed one to grieve but, if they could afford it, to hire others who would join them in loud sounds of lamentation as they carried the body to its final resting place. There was "a large crowd," the text says; the noise would have been both heartrending and earsplitting.

Jesus had compassion on the mother and, over the din of the mourners, said to her, "Do not weep."

Imagine saying that to a mother crying for her only son as he is about to be buried.

Then Jesus laid his hand on the bier, halting the bearers. "Young man," he said, addressing the corpse, "I say to you, rise!" Imagine that, too. What a crazy fellow! But the dead man sat up, just like that, and began speaking.

Fear fell on all the people, says the text, "And they glorified God, saying, 'God has looked favorably on his people!' "

Do you understand the theology of this? Jesus isn't merely a powerful wonder-worker. He is the Son of the living God, whose act of raising a man from the dead is a foretaste of what the reign of God is about. When God, who through Christ visited his people for a moment, is enthroned among them forever, there will be no more death and separation. Mothers will no longer take their sons to the cemetery, or husbands their wives, or citizens their friends. Death and mourning will be banished everlastingly, and there will be no need for tears.

I remember a beautiful phrase from Alfred North Whitehead, the great mathematician and philosopher, which I read so long ago that I can no longer recall the source. Whitehead defined the God of the universe as "a tender care that nothing be lost."

Think of that definition: God is "a tender care that nothing be lost."

It is a great saying, isn't it?

I thought of it when my mother died and was buried. She was gone from our sight, but she was not lost. God would see to that. I thought of it again when my father died. He, too, had gone "beyond the horizon." But again, he, too, was not lost. He was still held within the love of God.

So it is with everything we have loved or held dear. Our hearts may be made heavy by losing them for now, but they are not lost forever, because the God who is a "tender care that nothing be lost" will not suffer them to disappear for eternity. In this life, we grieve for what is gone. But in the life to come, in the anti-structures of God's reign, there will be no reason to grieve. Everything will reside safely and eternally in the presence of the One who created it.

My friend Richard Speight has written a touching little book of personal reminiscences entitled *The Pancake Man and Friends* (Dimensions for Living, 1992). In it, he tells the story of Willie the Weeper, a diminutive black man sent to Richard by a friend to help him and his wife Barbara clean up an old house they had bought. Willie was in his late sixties when the Speights met him. He had a shiny bald head and eyes that perpetually watered, giving him his nickname "the Weeper." He was a mysterious little fellow who never spoke of his background and refused to sleep in the house, where he was offered a bed. Instead, he spent his nights on an old mattress in the basement.

Willie was a prodigious worker. If told to dig a ditch through the yard, he might, if unsupervised for a short while, dig it all the way to the boundary of the property and continue into a neighbor's yard. Once, Richard was considering taking down a block wall that stood in his backyard. He asked Willie if he thought it would be hard to knock the wall down. He didn't say to do it; he was merely considering the possibility. A few minutes later, Richard came around the house and a ten-foot section of the wall was already lying broken up on the ground. Willie stood in the midst of the rubble with a proud grin on his face.

Willie worked for the Speights off and on for years. Sometimes he would appear at Richard's law office with some money he wanted deposited in an account. Other times he would come to withdraw some money. This is why, when Willie was mugged one night and then died of exposure, the police called Richard. They had found a scrap of paper with the name of his law firm in Willie's pocket.

Richard and Barbara took Willie's body to a funeral home and arranged for his services. Most of the mourners at Willie's funeral were black. They were strangers who had been recruited by the funeral director. The old black minister who conducted the service hadn't known Willie either. But Richard says he will never forget the words he spoke over Willie's body.

"Now, I didn't have the privilege of knowing the late Mister Hunter," he began. "I am certain that he was, in this life, a fine man. But whatever he was, I know for sure that he is now at home with his Maker, walking along those golden streets, somewhere beyond the purple hills of time."

"Amen," whispered Richard. "Amen."

God is "a tender care that nothing be lost."

Not even an old black man who came and went in people's lives, worked for them to earn a few dollars, and showed up when he needed something. Not even Willie the Weeper, whose last name Richard didn't know until the police told him after Willie died.

There is one more thing.

"Blessed are those who mourn," said Jesus, "for they will be comforted."

The Greek word for "comforted" is very long. It is *paraklethesontai.*

If you are quick, you will already have noticed that the root of this long word is the same as the English word we have taken from it, *paraclete,* which is used to speak of the Comforter or

Counselor or Holy Spirit Jesus promised to send among his disciples when he left them.

"I will ask the Father," Jesus told the disciples at the Last Supper, "and he will give you another Advocate, to be with you forever. This is the Spirit of truth, whom the world cannot receive, because it neither sees him nor knows him. You know him, because he abides with you, and he will be in you" (John 14:16-17). This Advocate would teach them "all things," and help them to remember everything Jesus had said (John 14:26).

When this Counselor came, said Jesus, he would

> show the world how wrong it was,
> about sin,
> and about who was in the right,
> and about judgement:
> about sin:
> in that they refuse to believe in me;
> about who was in the right:
> in that I am going to the Father
> and you will see me no more;
> about judgement:
> in that the prince of this world is already condemned.
>   (John 16:8-11 NJB)

There is the source of all the comfort: God is already active in the world to condemn the evil one, the prince of this world, and to set things right. God will overcome the tornness and brokenness of the divine creation—has been overcoming it already in Christ—and will one day reunite everything that belongs together into a single, joyous unity. Nothing will be lost. There will no longer be anything to cry over.

And the wonderful secret of Christ's followers is that they know this now. They are already experiencing this oneness through the Comforter, the Holy Spirit, who was given to the followers after Christ's death and resurrection. They are not immune to death and loss in this world. But they know that death and loss are not forever. They are already comforted by the thought that the mourning will end.

One of my favorite books in recent years has been a little paperback book I discovered on a used book stand in Oxford, England. It is called *The Pastor's Wife,* and it was written by Sabina Wurmbrand, the wife of Richard Wurmbrand, a Romanian minister who for years after World War II was imprisoned by the Communists. I know of few books from any age more impacted by Christian sentiment and absorbing life experiences.

After the war, the Wurmbrands took into their home a number of orphaned Jewish children from Eastern Romania and kept them as their own children, coming to love them dearly. But after the Soviets annexed two provinces of Romania and began repopulating them with refugees, the Wurmbrands feared that the children would be seized and taken to the Communist work camps, so they arranged for them to be transported to the new state of Israel. With tears and murmurs of love, the children were accordingly taken aboard the Turkish ship *Bulbul,* to be watched over by other refugees fleeing to Israel.

Days passed, and there was no news from the *Bulbul.* Search parties were sent out. Inquiries were made. The ship had not arrived in port. No one knew what had happened to it. At last it was concluded that the ship had hit a wartime mine and gone down with all souls aboard.

Sabina's faith was put to the test. She loved those children with all her heart. They were like her own. When it finally became evident that the ship had perished, she didn't want to speak to anyone. All her beliefs—in the Resurrection, in life after death, in the love of God—were questioned. Many times, she said, she thought she would never overcome the pain in her breast.

But at last, one day, the word of God slipped quietly into her heart, saying, "My peace I give unto you."

Suddenly everything was different. The old promises came back with new strength. She realized that God would not suffer his little ones to be lost forever. She became a tower of comfort to others, especially to her son Mihai, who still wept for his little brothers and sisters.

Then her husband Richard was imprisoned by the authorities. Sabina went to the officials, trying to find out what had happened to him, what would be done with him. She was one of hundreds of wives and children seeking loved ones who had been wrongfully incarcerated. The officials would divulge nothing. She did not know where Richard was or how to contact him. There was nothing to do but wait. Sometimes she wept, thinking that her dear husband might be undergoing torture at that very moment. As the wife of a political prisoner, she lost her ration card. She asked how she and Mihai were to live. "That's your business," said the officials.

"If Richard died," Sabina wrote, "I knew we would meet in the next life. We had agreed to wait for each other at one of the twelve gates of Heaven. We had decided that our rendezvous would be at the Benjamin Gate. Jesus made an appointment like this with his disciples, to meet them after his death, in Galilee. And He kept it" (London: Hodder & Stoughton, 1970, p. 37).

Then Sabina was imprisoned and sent to a work camp. She was endlessly questioned about her husband and the people they knew. Then she was simply forgotten, like all the other prisoners, and used for labor. She slept in a crowded barracks where hundreds of women had no privacy and only a little space to lie down at night. Summer and winter they worked in the fields until their skin was parched and their hands bled. Their food was a thin soup ladled into metal bowls. Some days they rejoiced if they found three beans in it instead of two. When someone died from work or overexposure, her bed was given to another prisoner.

During all these years, Sabina slept under a blanket that was special. Early in her imprisonment, she had worked loose a piece of chalky plaster from the wall in the barracks. She had used this to make the sign of the cross on her blanket. It was "in thankfulness," she said, for what God had done for her. It was also a sign of her hope.

"Blessed are those who mourn"—who are here separated from those they love most in all the world, and who must endure the indignities of human frailty and powerlessness—"for they will be comforted." Are *already* comforted, in fact, by the promises of Christ and the presence of the divine Spirit.

The reign of God is on its way.

Nothing will stop it.

And God is "a tender care that nothing be lost."

CHAPTER THREE

BLESSED
ARE THE
MEEK

Blessed are the meek, for they will inherit the earth" (Matt. 5:5).

Someone once reported finding these words inscribed on the wall of a lavatory in a British pub. The phrase "—if that's all right with the rest of you" was appended to them.

Meekness personified.

Mildness of manner.

Gentleness and retiringness.

Perhaps even servility.

In the Old Testament, especially in the Psalms, the word would have been *humble* or *obedient*. Blessed are the humble, the ones who are obedient to God's desires.

Here, in the New Testament, its meaning has to do with being under control, being submitted or disciplined, as a dog or a horse is said to be under control when it is trained to obey its master. Blessed are those who behave gently and well because they are disciplined in the manner of God.

I think of some of the genuinely meek people I have known.

My mother was a meek woman, as her father before her had been. My father was, on the contrary, a bull of a man, selfish and demanding, expecting the world to whirl magnetically around his needs and desires. At least he expected my mother to do so. And she did, as long ago as I can remember and until her dying day. It was always "Jess, do this" and "Jess, do that," and she leapt up from whatever she was doing, however important it was, to cater to his wishes.

For years my father carried on an affair with another woman. Sometimes he invited her to our home and ordered my mother to prepare dinner for her. She never refused. One afternoon when the three of them were sitting in our living room, my father announced that he wanted to divorce my mother and marry the other woman. My mother wept and said she loved him and did not want a divorce. They talked earnestly—and my father often abusively—for an hour, my mother weeping most of the time.

We had a number of goats then, and the hour came for the nannies to be milked. My father ordered my mother to go and see to the milking. I followed her to the barn, too young to be of any real assistance. She was snuffling most of the time as the goats' milk *skew-skawed, skew-skawed* into the milk buckets. I hated my father for the humiliation he was heaping upon my mother. But she never said a word against him, for she loved him dearly and herself not nearly enough.

She always had a strange kind of inner control, born partly of her personality and partly of her religious convictions. Raised in a Christian home, she believed there were certain kinds of behavior open to Christians and other kinds not open. A Christian, she believed, forgives and turns the other cheek. The meek shall inherit the earth.

Brother W. R. Munday was a meek man. He was one of the few African Americans I knew when I was growing up in a small town in Kentucky. A large man with a well-cultivated voice, Brother Munday was pastor of the A.M.E. Zion church in our community. The A.M.E. Zion church building was a small frame structure, painted white, that sat incongruously at the bottom of Harvey's Hill—a prestigious street of fine houses belonging to some of the town's most elite families—where it entered the town as Main Street. Most of the Caucasian citizens had never been in this building, but everyone had passed it on Saturday night and Sunday afternoon when the members were in high gear with their singing and when four or five deacons, dressed like pallbearers for a state funeral, were standing around the bottom of the steps out front smoking and swapping stories.

Brother Munday was not only pastor of this little church, he was also the janitor for two of the banks on the city square and several lesser establishments near the banks. On Saturday nights and Sundays, and occasionally when there was a funeral or wedding in his church, he wore a black suit and looked like a high-powered corporate lawyer; but from Monday through Saturday noon he could be found in or near one of these business houses in his work clothes.

Although he was large enough and probably strong enough to whip any man in a fair fight, Brother Munday was one of the gentlest and politest men I ever met, speaking softly and kindly to every man, woman, and child who passed him on the street. If his hands were free, he would tip his hat and bow slightly, always from somewhere deep inside, as if his soul were inclined before the idea ever reached his brain or his body, and he never failed to greet the people he met with a "ma'm" or "sir." When he called me "sir" and patted me on the arm, it always made me feel about ten feet tall.

After I became the pastor of a small church in the county, Brother Munday and I worked out an exchange whereby he preached in my church and I in his. This was a decade before the days of the freedom marches and racial integration, yet Brother Munday and his wife were so popular with the people of my church that they were asked to return again and again.

By this time, I was old enough to resent the injustice of Brother Munday's situation. He was the epitome of a scholar and a gentleman, yet earned his living emptying trash cans, mopping floors, and cleaning windows for people who often enough were unworthy to touch his shoestrings. While he and his wife lived in an extremely modest home and didn't own a car, there were ministers far inferior to him living in large, comfortable parsonages and driving expensive automobiles.

Yet never, in all the years I knew and loved this gentle man, did I hear him utter a single word of complaint, or even suggest, by the tone of his voice or the lifting of an eyebrow, that he was less than content and happy with the life God had given him to live.

We moved away and lived in other states and even other countries. But years later, when my mother died and I was conducting her burial service in the local cemetery, I looked up from the casket and saw his beautiful face, thinner and older now, his hair peppery-white, shining from the edge of the crowd. Afterward, we embraced and he told me how sorry he was about my mother's death, as they had been good friends. And then when my father died he was there again, even thinner and older, and walking somewhat feebly, and once more we held to each other and spoke of the things that touched us both.

That was the last time I saw Brother Munday. I thought he had died. But recently someone told me that he is living in a rest home. If I am still among the living, I hope someone notifies me when he dies and I am able to attend his funeral. I want to help celebrate his entering into the great reward he has so amply earned across the years.

He is one of God's genuinely meek souls—a deeply good and gentle man who is under the control of the divine Spirit, harnessed to bless the world and everyone whose life he touches.

What is the *opposite* of a meek person, one is led to ask. Numerous adjectives come to mind: swaggering, self-centered, boastful, assertive, aggressive, uncontrolled, undisciplined, wild, dangerous, ungodly.

Ungodly suggests an interesting notion. If ungodly is the opposite of meek, then meek is godly. This leads to the thought that God, the creator of the universe and source of all life, is meek.

In what way could that be true?

God is not a tyrant, reeling about in heavenly power and zapping mere mortals for the fun of it, the way the deities of ancient mythology often did. God is in touch with God's self, and conforms to God's own inner discipline. God does not behave wildly and erratically, without plan or pattern, without justice and mercy. It is God's nature to be gentle, loving, forgiving, healing, nurturing, building, atoning, and uniting.

When we are meek, therefore, we are imitating God. We are not retreating from confrontation and pressure. We are merely behaving in the peaceable manner of the divine nature itself.

This means that there is no contradiction between being meek and having power. I'm afraid we sometimes think such a contradiction exists. We imagine that one cannot be meek and aspire to political office or managerial status in a corporation or wealth and power in a community. But this is not true. Meekness is not a function of powerlessness and disconnectedness, but a function of a spiritual attitude, whatever one's power and position. In Judeo-Christian terms, it is a function of servanthood.

Gandhi understood this, and developed the idea of nonviolent resistance. He said he learned it from Jesus, the great teacher of Christianity.

Martin Luther King, Jr. understood it too and led his people in one of the greatest revolutions for human rights the world has ever known. He said he learned it from Jesus and Gandhi.

Now even the leading corporate thinkers of America are beginning to see the importance of meekness and to preach that management styles that serve employees are not only more moral than mere business-oriented styles but more practical and profitable as well. The systems within which people work, they say, function better when the people themselves are healthy, wholesome, and rewarded in spiritual ways for what they do. In these days of global competition, only the firms that care about the holistic patterns of employees' lives—including their families, personalities, and general well-being—will have the inner strength and will to survive.

Personal mastery is the phrase today's business gurus are using to describe what companies must aim at for their employees. When they define it, it is not far from the biblical idea of meekness, of having control of one's life and submitting it to a spiritual power above oneself.

"Personal mastery," says M.I.T. professor Peter M. Senge in his widely read book *The Fifth Discipline,* "goes beyond competence and skills, though it is grounded in competence and skills. It goes beyond spiritual unfolding or opening, although it requires spiritual growth. It means approaching one's life as a creative work, living life from a creative as opposed to a reactive viewpoint" (New York: Doubleday/Currency, 1990, p. 141).

Bill O'Brien, president of Hanover Insurance Company in Massachusetts, says that what companies must aim at for all their employees, from the bottom to the top, is "advanced maturity." Managers, he suggests, must redefine what they are doing. They must give up "the old dogma of planning, organizing, and controlling," and realize "the almost sacredness of their responsibility for the lives of so many people." Their fundamental task, as he sees it, is "providing the enabling conditions for people to lead the most enriching lives they can" (Bill O'Brien, "Advanced Maturity," pamphlet available from Hanover Insurance Company, 100 North Parkway, Worcester, MA 01605).

What a revolutionary turn this is for America's corporate life. Jesus' teachings about the importance of the inner life over external circumstances, ethical considerations above personal profit, and an existence that serves the community and the divine instead of the self have finally begun to find their way into the speeches and manuals of management experts, and to be touted not by preachers and religious teachers but by conference leaders and motivational speakers at business seminars all across the country. Apparently they have begun to believe it is really true that the meek shall inherit the earth and that Jesus, far from imposing an impossible set of rules on humanity from some ethereal height, actually described the kind of life-style and life-attitude that blesses and enriches everybody who comes in contact with it.

I have watched this happening in the university where I teach. President Thomas Corts, a lean, handsome corporate leader in his early fifties, has succeeded at his job with enviable élan. When he took the reins of the university, the endowment of the school totaled less than $10 million. Through personal charm, vision, and tenaciousness—all filtered through 70- and 80-hour work weeks—in seven years he drove that figure up to well over $100 million, with prospects of its soon hitting $150 million, all of which seems little short of miraculous for a church-related university of just over 4,000 students. Any administrator, at this point, might be justified in adopting the perspective of the rich man in Jesus' parable who, seeing abundant crops in his fields, decided it was time to put his feet up and "eat, drink, and be merry."

Not Tom Corts.

Considering the stewardship of the growing prestige and power of his university, he asked, "What can be done better to serve our several constituencies in this university, including not only the students, their families, our alumni, and our sponsors, but also the faculty and staff who work here as well?" The answer was to make the university a cooperative venture in which everyone—all of these groups, including faculty and staff—would be highly rewarded for participation in terms of personal growth, global understanding, and spiritual enrichment. A quality-improvement officer was added to the administrative staff. Seminars and colloquies sprang up all over the campus. Input was invited from every quarter. The faculty was challenged to invent a new curriculum for the next century, one that would facilitate professional growth in the teachers as well as learning among the students. Staff members in the entire system, including secretaries and custodians, were encouraged to offer their suggestions for improving our common life.

Now the university throbs with a new hope and a new sense of mission. The spirit of volunteerism has shot up 100 percent. People are excited, for they know they are contributing to their own community, to the broadening and enriching of their own existence. The worth of personal contributions is no longer calculated in mere monetary terms. Now there is a sense of excitement on the campus that takes precedence over greed and self-interest. People *want* to be a part of what is happening. They can feel something growing that is fresh and stimulating and meaningful. Like the first Christians, they are ready to share what they have for the good of the whole.

Tom Corts is what I would call a meek leader.

This doesn't mean he is weak and deferential.

On the contrary, he is strong and inspiring. He is translating his understanding of the Christian faith into terms that actually produce results in the marketplace. He is using his position of power and influence to put the principles of Jesus into practice where they matter most, in the lives of ordinary people in the place where they spend the majority of their hours living, working, and interacting.

Let's return to the servanthood motif (actually we have never left it).

This is surely at the heart of what Jesus meant by being meek. As powerful and lordly as he was, Jesus came among us as a meek man, "self-emptied" for the glory of God, one who saw his mission as serving others instead of having them serve him. He refocused attention from the rich and powerful of his nation to the little people, the simple folk, even the outcasts of society. He told stories about unpretentious householders—a woman looking for the coin she lost, a boy who left home and came back, a shepherd who lost a sheep, a poor man who died and went to heaven, a man who was rewarded for giving a cup of water in his Lord's name. He praised a poor widow who came to the Temple and gave two small coins, all she had, for the relief of the poor. He defended prostitutes and tax-collectors against the arid self-righteousness of the religiously proper.

He talked about turning the other cheek, going the second mile, and praying for those who persecute us.

Once, when some folks got the idea of starting a movement that would make him an earthly king, Jesus slipped away to be alone and to pray. While he commended the use of riches to help the poor, he himself never had much in the way of earthly goods—apparently not even a home to call his own or an extra change of raiment. When he was preparing to leave his closest friends, he took a bowl of water and a towel and got down on his knees to wash their feet, insisting that they learn to live through serving one another, not by sitting in the places of honor. Betrayed by a follower who led the police to his prayer spot in Gethsemane, he kissed the follower and bade his friends not to raise their swords. Brought before Pilate and Caiaphas, he saw the uselessness of protest and fell into creative silence. Crucified between two criminals, he spoke kindly to the one with an open heart and forgave the soldiers who had followed orders in carrying out his execution.

He didn't have to be this way.

He didn't have to submit to such mistreatment.

The Gospel writers wanted us to know this. They suggested in several ways what a powerful man he was, and how he might have been a ruler if he had chosen to be, and how he could even have called down angels to take his side in Gethsemane. But, for all of this, he was a meek man, a man after the heart of God, a man *from* the heart of God. He didn't count himself or his own life as having that much importance. He came among us as a servant, as one seeking to honor God and make things better for others. Therefore he didn't save himself.

And he counseled against our trying to do so too.

"Unless a grain of wheat falls into the earth and dies," he said, "it remains just a single grain; but if it dies, it bears much fruit" (John 12:24).

Maybe that's what he meant by "inheriting" the earth. Not that the meek will own it or possess it the way people currently own or possess property. But that they will join it, become part of it, be united to the entire process of growth and community and well-being in the world.

That, as we are beginning to see, is far better than owning anything.

CHAPTER FOUR

BLESSED ARE THOSE WHO HUNGER AND THIRST FOR RIGHTEOUSNESS

Blessed are those who hunger and thirst for righteousness, for they will be filled" (Matt. 5:6).

I felt sorry for the man. He was a small-store owner in a deteriorating section of the city. He had been robbed four times in one month. Each time, the police had come around, asked a lot of questions, looked over the store, taken some fingerprints, and left. He knew it was useless to hope the culprits would be apprehended. At last, in desperation, he rigged up an explosive device in his storeroom. The next time there was a break-in, one of the robbers was badly hurt. This time the police arrested the store owner. He couldn't understand why he wasn't permitted to defend his own property.

We have a friend sixty-three years old who works for a large insurance company in California. A few months ago, a twenty-seven-year-old man was put in charge of her department. He wants to surround himself with people his age, and seems unable to conceive that anyone over forty should be employable any longer. He puts impossible requirements on our friend, obviously hoping she will leave so he can replace her with a younger person. She is miserable but cannot quit because she knows how hard it would be to find another job at her age. "It isn't fair," she says. "I often have to work until eight or nine at night to finish the tasks he assigns. But I know if I don't do them he will find an excuse to get rid of me."

The young boy in an express lube shop was complaining about the way he had been treated at a nearby garage. His car had recently gone out of warranty when he began having engine trouble. The manager at the garage told him he needed certain repair work done. The work had been done and he had paid for it, rather dearly. A week later, the problem had returned. He went back to the garage. They said he needed something else done. Again he agreed to the work and paid a large bill. Again the problem came back. The boy talked with the manager. It didn't seem right to him, he said, to keep paying for work that didn't solve his problem. The manager said he agreed, but they had their policies and one of them was that money would not be refunded on work that had been completed. Finally the boy took his car to another garage, where a mechanic diagnosed the problem as something very simple and inexpensive to fix. "I spent a lot of money I couldn't afford to spend," said the boy. "And there's nothing I can do about it."

Three women sat in a rape clinic talking about what had happened to them. One was a college girl whose boyfriend had forced her to have sex in her dorm room. She had screamed, but it was at lunchtime and apparently no one else was near her room. Another had been attacked as she was unloading groceries from her car at her apartment house. The third was an older woman who lived in a poor section of town. Her assailant had broken into her house in the middle of the night, raped her, struck her on the head, and stole her money, some silver, and a television set. The worst part, they all agreed, was how afraid they were. Two were afraid they might get AIDS. All three were afraid to go anywhere or even to be at home alone. The world now seemed like a jungle to them, with danger around every corner.

A woman from El Salvador worked as a housekeeper in a church I pastored. In El Salvador she had been trained as a social worker. She held the equivalent of a master's degree in her field. She had fled to the United States because her brother had been on the wrong side of the political situation in El Salvador, and her life was in danger if she remained there. She was not allowed to work as a social worker in the United States because she did not have the right kind of permit. She could not get this permit until she had been cleared by the government to immigrate here. The government was reluctant to give her the clearance because she could not actually prove she was in danger in her own country. So she worked as a housekeeper for minimum wages and paid exorbitant sums of money to a lawyer who specialized in helping refugees complete the difficult paperwork required by the government agencies investigating such cases.

A beautiful little girl was shown crying on a television program. The social workers had just removed her from her home because her mother and father were both drug addicts and the mother often beat her. There were bruises on the girl's head and arms where she had been struck. But she was terrified of being taken away by strangers. In her simple, childlike way, she preferred being with the parents who mistreated her to being trundled off to an institution in the custody of people she did not know.

This is not a perfect world. Far from it.

People suffer cruelties and injustices all the time.

Inequities abound.

Evil and crime seem to permeate the very fabric of human existence.

So there are an awful lot of people hungering and thirsting after righteousness. Wanting things to be okay. Wishing the world were full of honesty and compassion and fairness. Longing for the kind of life promised by the anti-structures of God.

The Bible is plain about one thing.

The kind of righteousness and fairness we are talking about comes from only one source, and that source is God.

God is the God of righteousness.

In the Old Testament, and in the New Testament world that grew out of the Old Testament view of things, there is no substitute. God is the one. All righteousness springs from the heavenly Father, however much we would like to pretend otherwise.

The Hebrew word for righteousness, *tsedeq*, appears more than five hundred times in the Old Testament. Its counterpart in Greek, *dikaiosune*, appears more than two hundred times in the New Testament. It is a central concept of the Bible. God is righteous, upright, filled with justice. This would almost seem to be the very core of God.

"Praise the LORD according to his righteousness," says Psalm 7:17 (KJV). "He shall judge the world in righteousness," adds Psalm 9:8 (KJV). God leads us "in paths of righteousness," says familiar Psalm 23:3 (KJV). "The heavens declare his righteousness," attests Psalm 97:6 (KJV). God's city shall be called "the city of righteousness," says Isaiah 1:26. "The LORD is our righteousness," declares Jeremiah 23:6 and 33:16. We are to "strive first for the kingdom of God and his righteousness," says Matthew 6:33. Grace itself reigns through righteousness, adds the Apostle Paul in Romans 5:21.

Sometimes we use the word *righteousness* in a pejorative sense, implying a kind of stuffiness or sanctimoniousness. This is especially true if we add the word *self* to it. Self-righteousness is a particularly negative quality. It offends our sensibilities.

But God's righteousness is not negative at all. If it implies condemnation of any kind, that is because unrighteousness is naturally condemned when it stands in the presence of righteousness. God's righteousness or holiness is actually the most positive thing in the world. On a smaller scale, it is like the goodness or uprightness of a human being we know. I think of a wonderful friend of mine who is so disciplined to do the right thing, to take the high road, to think the best thoughts, that it is inconceivable to me that she would ever do anything low or mean or despicable. It is as if there were a core of goodness in her, something at the very center of her being that radiates out into every thought and action, that makes her an unflagging source of justice and wisdom to everyone around her. This is the way it is with God. God is righteous by God's very nature. All goodness and holiness and mercy proceed from God because of this. God makes everything better merely because God exists. If God did not exist, the moral universe would be plunged instantly into darkness and hopelessness.

The only reason the world is as hard a place as it is, with manifestations of evil and cruelty and injustice wherever we turn, is because people down through the ages have chosen to reject God instead of setting the divine righteousness in their midst and letting it permeate all human affairs.

What a different world it would be if the dream of the prophets had long ago been fulfilled, that all the nations should fall down and acknowledge God as the Divine Ruler, structuring their lives, their businesses, their relationships, their politics, everything, according to the divine Spirit. But the world is not a simple place. It is divided in its allegiances. Part of it resists goodness and justice, and supports wrongdoing and inequities.

The Bible explains this as the work of Satan, the archenemy of God's purposes. Many people in our sophisticated age think of Satan as a mythological being, like Zeus or Hermes or Athena. He doesn't really exist, they say; he is only the personification of evil, which is an abstract quality. Jesus and the early Christians took Satan seriously, though. We need to remember that in the fourth chapter of Matthew's Gospel, only a few verses prior to the Sermon on the Mount, is the story of Jesus' being led into a wilderness place where he was tempted by the devil. While his struggles with the devil are possibly generic or categorical—that is, they represent "types" of trials through which Christians pass—they are nevertheless presented as real-life, you'd-better-believe-it struggles, struggles on which the validity of the rest of Jesus' ministry would depend.

Later, Jesus would tell a parable about God's reign that likened it to the good seed a farmer sowed in a field. But during the night an enemy came and sowed weeds in the field as well, so that the good plants, when they appeared, were in places almost choked out by weeds. The farmer's helpers were distressed and asked if he wanted them to pull up the weeds. He said no, there was too much likelihood of ruining some of the plants that were good. They would wait until the harvest time, and then the two would be separated and the weeds destroyed (Matt. 13:24-30).

Sensible management.

And a good picture of the way it is with God's righteousness in the world. Someone has marred what God intended by sowing weeds among the good plants. But the weeds have not choked out the righteousness, even though they exist side by side for the present time. In the judgment, they will be appropriately dealt with. For now, we can merely hunger and thirst for the day.

Sometimes it isn't easy to put up with such an arrangement.

"Sliding down the razor blade of life," someone has called it. Putting up with crime and cruelty and injustice and greed and pollution and mismanagement and all the rest, while we dream of parity and love and justice and honesty and peace and dependability and all those other good things.

Nevertheless, said Jesus, "blessed are those who hunger and thirst for righteousness, for they shall be postponed."

No, not postponed.

" . . . for they shall be bought off."

No, not bought off.

" . . . for they shall be mollified."

No, not mollified.

" . . . for they shall be *satisfied*."

Ah, that is something.

Satisfied.

Filled.

Have enough of something.

It is the Greek verb *chortazo,* which appears also in Mark 8:4, when Jesus is out in the wilderness with a great crowd of people who have nothing to eat. The disciples want to send them home, but Jesus says he has compassion on them and will feed them. The disciples want to know how he can possibly satisfy (*chortasai*) them there in the desert. Jesus collects the few loaves of bread and fishes they have, gives thanks for them, and begins breaking them for the disciples to distribute to the people. "And they ate," says verse 8, "and were satisfied [*echortasthesan*] (KJV)." They were filled.

In the desert.

Wow! What a powerful vision of what the Christian faith is about. People hungering and thirsting for something that seems almost impossible in the world. But Jesus gives it right there where it is hardest to do it. He provides what everybody is looking for, so that everybody is filled. Right in the desert.

Obviously this is all tied in with the mystery of how the rule of God can have come in Christ and still not be over-whelmingly evident every place we look. The anti-structures are here, but they are yet to come. The kingdom is among us, but the people I talked about at the beginning of this chap-ter—the robbed store owner, the woman in the insurance company, the boy whose car needed repairing, the women in the rape clinic, the refugee from El Salvador, the girl being taken away from her parents—have a hard time seeing it.

How can we explain this? How can the new rule of God be here in Christ if the old evils are still rampant everywhere we look?

Perhaps I can illustrate it with what is happening just now at the university where I teach. A new age is dawning for our university. We have a beautiful campus. There are many wonderful professors. There is an abundance of students. Things were moving along peacefully, without any new thing occurring on the campus. Then, two or three years ago, the administrators got the dream of making the university one of the best small universities in the nation. They talked with a man noted for his work in quality improvement for education. His ideas were so stimulating that he was hired to become the assistant provost and begin implementing them.

At first the faculty members were resistant. They weren't sure they wanted any wave of change to sweep through the university—especially if it affected them and their departments. But gradually the new leader's ideas began to take hold. Little groups here and there on the campus talked with new excitement about what was happening. Then the time came for an entirely new curriculum to be set in place. Many faculty members worked long, hard hours to develop it. Then many more faculty members worked long, hard hours to prepare the actual courses to be taught. A large group of students became part of the pilot project to test the new materials. By this time, the excitement about change was almost at fever pitch in the university. Outwardly, everything looked pretty much the same. But everyone knew that something big and important was in the offing, that enormous change was coming. The anti-structures, the framework for a new era, were here, right on our campus, although they had not outwardly begun to show.

Isn't this how it is with Christ?

Christ didn't immediately overturn the evil in the world. In fact, he was crucified by it.

But the *logos* of the new rule—the word, the shape, the idea—had appeared with him, and it was beginning to defeat evil. This is what all the miracles of Jesus were about. They were not gratuitous episodes of muscle-flexing. They were signs of the power of the new age, when the poor would be fed, the diseased healed, the lame made to walk, the blind given sight, even the dead raised. They were, in the words of the old hymn, "foretastes of glory divine."

In the meantime, while the rule of God is coming, Christ is the measure of that rule, and the condemnation of everything that does not measure up to it. As the New Adam, he is the picture of what God really intended for humanity—the wisdom and love and obedience and creativeness and purity and goodness and everything else. The very fact that we have known him, that he has lived and walked in our midst, that we have his teachings and have been instructed to follow him, yet have not done so very faithfully, becomes our judgment.

In Herman Melville's *Moby Dick,* the great novel about the American whaling industry of the nineteenth century, there is an unforgettable passage about a ship's lantern that hung in the captain's room on the *Pequod.* No matter which way the ship yawed and hawed in the rolling, pitching waves, the lantern always hung down exactly perpendicular to a line drawn through the center of the earth. As Melville said, it "revealed the false, lying levels" of everything around it.

So it is with Christ.

When Christ enters the boardroom of a church, he instantly uncovers the shoddiness of Christian practice among those charged with following his way.

When Christ enters the halls of politics, he reveals the self-interest and mismanagement affecting those who conduct the business of government.

When Christ enters a bank or an insurance company or a hospital or a law office, he lays bare the failure of people to live by God's standards and desires.

When Christ enters the room with one of us, he inevitably shows up our shortcomings and makes us want to fall on our knees and ask forgiveness.

This is all necessary before the reign of God has fully come. It is an unwritten rule of everything God does that judgment precedes God's full disclosure of grace and redemption to those who wait for them. This is why John the Baptist came in advance of Jesus, preaching repentance and renewal before the

Lord himself should arrive. It is like the sultry wind that begins to whip the leaves of the tree before the storm arrives. It says, "Something big is coming, you should prepare."

The "big" thing that is coming is described by John in the book of Revelation. He says:

> Then one of the seven angels who had the seven bowls came and said to me, "Come, I will show you the judgment of the great whore who is seated on many waters, with whom the kings of the earth have committed fornication, and with the wine of whose fornication the inhabitants of the earth have become drunk." So he carried me away in the spirit into a wilderness, and I saw a woman sitting on a scarlet beast that was full of blasphemous names, and it had seven heads and ten horns. The woman was clothed in purple and scarlet [for both royalty and harlotry], and adorned with gold and jewels and pearls, holding in her hand a golden cup full of abominations and the impurities of her fornication; and on her forehead was written a name, a mystery: "Babylon the great, mother of whores and of earth's abominations." And I saw that the woman was drunk with the blood of the saints and the blood of the witnesses to Jesus. (Rev. 17:1-6)

The beast will be cast into perdition, says John (Rev. 17:8), and the great harlot will suffer a resounding fall. Plagues will come upon her

> "in a single day—
> pestilence and mourning and famine—
> and she will be burned with fire;
> for mighty is the Lord God who judges her."

And the kings of the earth, who committed fornication and lived in luxury with her, will weep and wail over her when they see the smoke of her burning; they will stand far off, in fear of her torment, and say,

> "Alas! alas! the great city,
> Babylon, the mighty city!
> For in one hour your judgment has come." (Rev. 18:8-10)

We should regard this interim period before the great harlot has been destroyed and the reign of God has fully arrived as a grace time, a time for preparing ourselves and the world around us. Here is our true motivation for evangelism in the modern world. God has given us this segment of life between the initial coming of the kingdom and its full arrival to spread the word about it, to conform ourselves to the image of the Son, and to hold up that image to others; so that the world itself will be prepared for what lies ahead.

John hears another voice from heaven urging people to flee from the harlot. It says:

> "Come out of her, my people,
>   so that you do not take part in her sins,
> and so that you do not share in her plagues;
> for her sins are heaped high as heaven,
>   and God has remembered her iniquities." (Rev. 18:4-5)

God clearly wants people to escape the judgment, to become like Christ, and to be at home in the divine rule before it has arrived as final, cataclysmic condemnation.

When the new age has fully come, it will be an age of righteousness. Disparities and injustices will have flown away with the dawn. A spirit of peace and gentleness will settle over all who remain, those who have not been destroyed by hatred and greed and lust and contempt. All life will be caught up in songs of praise to the Creator-Redeemer. The evil one, "the dragon, that ancient serpent, who is the Devil and Satan," will be seized, bound, and thrown into the pit (Rev. 20:2-3). Then, after a period in which he is allowed to roam once more in the world, gathering his forces for battle, he and all his followers will be thrown into a lake of fire, where they will burn forever and ever (Rev. 20:7-10). God will reign eternally on the throne at the heart of all existence, with Christ, the model of the new humanity, at his side.

Then the hunger and thirst of all God's people for righteousness will be satisfied. The promises will be fulfilled. There will be no more poverty, disease, despair, crime, injustice, disparity, blindness, deafness, lameness, stress, anxiety, loneliness, alienation, discrimination, abuse, bitterness, or cynicism. God will be all in all, and all his people will look upon his face and sing endless praises to him in a land where there will never again be darkness.

That will be blessedness—happiness—beyond all description!
But what about the present?

Well, the story of a friend of mine may help.

He was president of a banking institution. During a volatile period, some of the board members became restless and decided they should put him out and get a new president. They sprang it on him suddenly. He was informed at 4:00 P.M. one afternoon that they had voted him out, and he was to clear all personal effects out of his office by the time he left that evening. He was completely stunned.

In the days that followed, his former friends on the board would have nothing to do with him. He and his wife were totally ostracized. The local newspapers were often filled with stories about the changes at the institution. Then word came that there might have been some financial improprieties, and the government was investigating. More newspaper stories. My friend had to hire an expensive lawyer to defend his name. Eventually the case against him was dismissed and his name cleared. But not before he and his wife had gone through a terrible ordeal of shame and loneliness in the community.

I knew this man well. His character was beyond reproach. He had been sandbagged and betrayed by friends on the board. It was all a horrible act of injustice that hurt an innocent man wrongly and unnecessarily.

One afternoon I was sitting with him in his living room, talking about what had transpired and how he and his family were doing. It was a quiet time. I was aware of the ticking of several antique clocks around the room.

"How are you feeling right now?" I asked.

He thought for only a second or two.

"I am both very miserable and very happy," he said. "I am miserable because of what we are going through, but I am also happy because I know that I am not guilty and that God will one day straighten out this old mess of a world."

That is pretty much where all of us are at this point of our existence. The sin and injustice around us make us miserable. But knowing that God is going to straighten it all out makes us happy.

The trick of Christian living is to meditate so much on what makes us happy that the misery doesn't get us down.

CHAPTER FIVE

BLESSED
ARE THE
MERCIFUL

Blessed are the merciful, for they will receive mercy" (Matt. 5:7).

What sort of person *isn't* merciful?

I think of someone bitter, grudging, unwilling to compromise, wanting to exact full payment for a wrong, inwardly corroded by the acids of vengeance.

Sometimes it is the man who has never been able to forgive his father for humiliating or hurting him when he was a boy, and carries a bitterness in his heart for the rest of his life, always speaking of his father contemptuously and disclosing the fact that he himself is filled with frustration, resentment, and the wish that he could get even.

Sometimes it is the woman who always felt like an outsider with her friends when she was growing up, and envied their clothes, their manners, their happy-go-lucky attitudes. Because she has never dealt successfully with her conflicts, her blood pressure still rises when she thinks of these companions.

Sometimes it is the veteran who lost a limb or was badly scarred in battle and has never stopped resenting being marked in this way by a war he didn't choose. He may even secretly hate God for having made the kind of world where wars exist and young men go to fight enemies on foreign soil and come home maimed and crippled for the rest of their lives.

Sometimes it is the person who has been continually denied the job he or she wants, or has been passed over for an honor by someone he or she deems inferior and unworthy of it, or has never been recognized and rewarded as a person of value. The hurt is like a barb that continually twists and festers in the inner spirit, producing pain and infection and unhappiness.

What did the elder brother say, in the parable of the prodigal son, when the father entreated him to come into the house and join the celebration over the lost son's return? "You have never given me even a young goat so that I might celebrate with my friends" (Luke 15:29).

Envy.

Frustration.

Bitterness.

An inability to be filled with mercy.

Jesus knew the meanness of the human condition—how people nurse their inner wounds and carry grudges for years, and try to sabotage friends and relatives who are being happy, and look for bizarre ways of wreaking vengeance long after some initial harm was done to them. He saw it all around him, in friends, in his followers, perhaps even in his parents and brothers and sisters. He understood how it settles like a fog on the individual spirit, shutting out the vision of God and the sense of elation and generosity that vision always produces.

All through his ministry, therefore, he talked about love, forgiveness, mercy, nonretaliation, canceling debts, and reestablishing communion.

Once Simon Peter—that hard, aggressive fellow who probably grew up thinking forgiveness was a lot of rubbish and that you have to be firm with people or they will take advantage of you— had heard so much about mercy and love that he wanted to be sure he was hearing the Master correctly. "Lord, how often shall my brother sin against me, and I forgive him?" he asked. "As many as seven times?"

Perhaps Peter thought even this figure was stretching the point, and that Jesus would say, "Oh, I didn't mean all that much. Maybe a couple of times. Then you can confront him and see that he shapes up."

But Jesus didn't.

Jesus said, "Not seven times, but, I tell you, seventy-seven times" (Matt. 18:22).

It was a rhetorical answer.

It didn't mean precisely seventy-seven times.

It meant, "You haven't even begun to get warm. Time after time after time. More times than you want to count. So many times that you can't possibly remember the wrong by the time you reach it."

And then Jesus told the story of the king who wanted to settle accounts with his servants. In the course of doing so, the king discovered that one man owed him an astronomical sum—ten thousand talents. A single talent was worth all a laboring man could earn in fifteen years. So this man's debt was worth 150 thousand years of work. It was like a national debt! He couldn't possibly begin to pay it.

Faced with being sold into slavery—with his wife and children—the man begged for mercy.

The king, taking pity on him, released him and forgave the debt. Wiped out 150 thousand years of work's worth of indebtedness. What a wonderful king!

But that isn't the end of the story.

The newly forgiven man went out through the king's courtyard. On his way, he spied a fellow who owed *him* some money. A hundred denarii, to be precise. The denarius was worth a single day's labor by a common man. A hundred denarii was not an inconsiderable debt, for it was all a laboring person could earn in 100 days. Yet it was infinitesimal compared to the debt this man himself had so recently been forgiven.

Apparently he forgot what the king had done for him. He had a short memory and a shallow sense of gratitude. He had failed to be transformed by the great mercy shown to him. Seizing the other man by the throat—a vicious, compelling gesture—he demanded that the other man pay up. When the man pled for patience, he had none. Instead, he called the bailiffs and had the man thrown into prison.

A great picture of human irony.

But the story still isn't over.

Word got back to the king about the forgiven man's behavior. The king was furious. How could anyone have such a lopsided understanding of justice? Summoning the man back to his court, the king said, "You wicked slave! I forgave you all that debt because you pleaded with me. Should you not have had mercy on your fellow slave, as I had mercy on you?" (Matt. 18:32-33).

And in his rage over the man's lack of fairness, the king had him thrown into prison until he could pay his entire debt, an outcome whose likelihood was probably less than one in ten million.

"So," said Jesus, "my heavenly Father will also do to every one of you, if you do not forgive your brother or sister from your heart" (Matt. 18:35).

Not even the appearance of forgiveness is enough.

It must come from the heart.

In the presence of God, there must be a total, consistent attitude of love and mercy. Anything else is insufficient, for it is unworthy of the God who is loving and merciful by God's own nature.

Perhaps this is a good place to pause and reflect on the possible relation of this beatitude to the one that preceded it, about those who "hunger and thirst for righteousness." In what way is mercy or forgiveness related to the desire for righteousness? It could be argued, from the foregoing parable, that the servant who had his fellow servant cast into prison for failure to pay his debt was merely taking into his hands the responsibility for creating a more just and righteous environment.

Yet the king was very upset with the man's behavior, for it showed no recognition of the great mercy he himself had enjoyed from the king.

Now the king himself was not reprimanded for having the first servant thrown into prison as a judgment against the man for being unmerciful. He was the king, and he could do whatever he wished. It is perhaps pushing the parable a bit to say so, but there is a sense in which he was above judgment.

By the same token, God is the one responsible for final judgment in the world. The outcome of that is left in God's hands, and we are promised that the hunger and thirst for righteousness will be satisfied.

But we, in the meantime, are to be merciful. As God has shown mercy on us by not destroying us for our sin and ineffectiveness, so we are to learn to have forgiveness in our hearts for other human beings who don't live up to our standards for their behavior. Even though we yearn for righteousness to triumph in the world, it is not up to us to force that triumph. Our disgust and contempt for unrighteousness are to be overshadowed by the sense of humility and gratitude that causes us to be generous and forgiving with the very persons around us who are contributing to the general state of unrighteousness.

This is of course very hard, until we learn to live in the Spirit and discover the joy of being channels of grace and mercy. The old Hebrew law, "An eye for an eye and a tooth for a tooth," was very expressive of the natural human instinct for enforcing a certain righteousness in human affairs.

But Jesus said:

> Do not resist an evildoer. But if anyone strikes you on the right cheek, turn the other also; and if anyone wants to sue you and take your coat, give your cloak as well; and if anyone forces you to go one mile, go also the second mile. Give to everyone who begs from you, and do not refuse anyone who wants to borrow from you. (Matt. 5:39-42)

At first this sounds like a prescription for personal disaster. Imagine not standing up to people who are evil, or giving people who take us to court even more than they want. How can anyone really live this way?

As difficult as such sayings appear, though, they need to be viewed in the light of Jesus' words about having mercy and being filled with that spontaneous joy that proceeds from realizing that God is in control of the world and will make everything work out for the best.

When I was only fifteen or sixteen years old, I heard Dr. Wayne Dehoney tell a story about a soldier that deeply impressed me and has continued to affect my attitudes and behavior to this day. Dehoney was talking about turning the other cheek and how absurd that kind of selflessness can seem to be until we understand how it affects others. It was only a few years after World War II, and many people in his audience had been in the army.

This fine young private, he said, had been a Christian for only a short time. But he was very committed to his faith and, in his commitment, read his Bible faithfully every day and tried to live

83

as he thought Jesus wanted him to live. This seemed to put him crosswise with a rough old sergeant who had nothing but contempt for Christianity and constantly gave the young man extra duties as a punishment for what he assumed was the naïveté of his faith. The young man was so sustained by his beliefs, however, that he always responded to the sergeant in a pleasant, cheerful manner, which only further infuriated the sergeant.

One rainy night when everyone had a pass to go into the nearby town, the private decided to remain behind to write some letters and read his Bible. He passed a quiet, uneventful evening in the barracks and was concluding it with a season of prayer when the sergeant, tired and drunk, stumbled through the door and saw him on his knees beside his bunk.

Angry and cursing, the sergeant pulled off his muddy boots, hurled them at the young soldier—striking him on both the head and the body—and fell into a stupor on his cot.

The next morning, when the sergeant awoke with a throbbing headache and a mouth that felt as if it were full of fuzz, he noted that someone had removed his tie, loosened his collar, and carefully laid a blanket across his body. And there beside his bed sat his boots, cleaned and polished with the best shine they had probably ever had.

I think the sergeant became a Christian after that. I don't remember. But I'll never forget the power of this picture of a human being managing a hateful, unrighteous situation by meeting it not with force but with love, not with defensive or aggressive behavior but with mercy and forgiveness.

I said that Jesus talked continually about love and mercy and forgiveness. But of course he didn't only talk about them. He enacted them. He embodied them. He showed us, in his own behavior, what they are all about.

What more complete picture of the merciful life could there be than the one Jesus gave us in the final hours of his life, when the pressures and stresses were greatest upon him?

Talk about not resisting evil. He kissed the man who was betraying him and urged his followers not to take up arms in his defense. He stood in regal silence before the high priest who was questioning him and again before Pilate, the Roman governor. He endured the punishment and indignities of the soldiers in the praetorium and submitted to an ignominious death on the cross, dying like a common criminal. Even in the very throes of death, when words were at a premium, he asked the Father in heaven to forgive the men who had crucified him, saying that they didn't know what they had done.

And afterwards, when he had been raised from death and was not in the tomb, the women who came out to anoint the body were instructed by the angel, "Go, tell his disciples and Peter that he is going ahead of you to Galilee; there you will see him" (Mark 16:7). Note the words *and Peter*. On the night before the crucifixion, Peter had denied even knowing Jesus. He had not only denied it, he had denied it vehemently, to save himself.

Who do you suppose instructed the angel to include Peter's name so prominently and individually in the directions given to the women? It would have been like Jesus, wouldn't it? And certainly afterwards, when they were all reunited in Galilee, Jesus went out of his way to assure Peter of his reinstatement in the fellowship. He took him aside and asked him three times how much he loved him—once for each time Peter had sworn he didn't know him. It was a beautiful, dramatic moment of forgiveness.

"Blessed are the merciful, for they will receive mercy." Happy are those who forgive others easily; they will find forgiveness as easily as they give it.

I think about a friend who years ago, at a time when she was very lonely and vulnerable, had a daughter by a man who would not marry her. A few years later, the man married another woman. Yet our friend never hated him for it. She shared the daughter with him, and taught her to love her father. When the man and his wife had children, she and the daughter sometimes went to baby-sit for them so they could get away for an evening out or even a brief vacation. When the couple needed money, she often gave them help, even though she and her daughter were barely making out on her modest salary. And when the daughter graduated from high school, she invited the father to come as her guest and sit with her for the special occasion, so the daughter would feel that her whole family was there.

It could have worked out quite differently. The woman could have been angry with the man and vowed never to have anything to do with him after he deserted her. She could have taught the daughter to hate him, and prevented her ever visiting him.

Knowing the woman, and what a lovely spirit she has, I realize how much poorer she would be today if she had allowed the hurt and brokenness to master her feelings. Instead, her beauty and generosity have grown through her sweet and gentle behavior. She lives with a sense of joy, seeing the refracted glory of God in many little things each day. Everyone who knows her speaks of her inner radiance, and no one could ever be resentful or angry with her. She is forgiven as easily as she has forgiven. She lives in an aura of mercy.

This woman is Dutch. Perhaps that is why she reminds me of Corrie ten Boom, another loving and forgiving Dutch woman, whose story of love and courage is known around the world.

In *The Hiding Place,* Corrie tells how she and her sister Betsy were interned at the Nazi camp at Ravensbruck. Betsy died there, and Corrie dreaded the day when, after the war, she might encounter one of their captors. It happened one day in Munich, where Corrie was giving her testimony at a rally. There was a former S.S. officer there who had stood guard at the showers in the camp. Corrie looked up and suddenly he was facing her.

"How grateful I am for your message, fraulein," he said. "To think that, as you say, He has washed my sins away!"

The man thrust out his hand to Corrie, but she could not take it. She felt shame and guilt coursing through her body. "Lord Jesus," she prayed, "forgive me and help me to forgive him." But nothing happened. There was no warmth or forgiveness in her.

Again she prayed: "Jesus, I cannot forgive him; give me Your forgiveness."

Struggling with herself, she took the man's hand. And as she did, she says "the most incredible thing happened. From my shoulder along my arm and through my hand a current seemed to pass from me to him, while into my heart sprang a love for this stranger that overwhelmed me" (Minneapolis: World Wide Press, 1971, p. 233).

There it is, just as Jesus said. The person who lives with mercy will have mercy. When Corrie realized how much she owed to Christ's mercy and turned to that in her hour of confrontation, she found that mercy flooding through her so abundantly that she could share it even with a man who had been a detestable enemy.

Mercy begets mercy.

It becomes a way of life.

And, when it does, it includes us in the very same way we reach out to include others.

Maybe this is why Jesus told the disciples, when they prayed, to say, "Forgive us our wrongs as we forgive those who wrong us" (Matt. 6:12, my translation).

Mercy is a package deal.

CHAPTER SIX

BLESSED
ARE THE
PURE IN HEART

Blessed are the pure in heart, for they will see God" (Matt. 5:8).

An apparently innocent, beautiful statement, right?

Wrong.

It is one of the most revolutionary things Jesus ever said, for he said it in the midst of a nation literally obsessed with purification laws and procedures.

Think about the legal codes of the Jews.

There were extensive rules about which creatures might and might not be eaten. Jews could eat cattle but could not eat camels, badgers, hares, and swine (Lev. 11:2-8). They could eat fish, but not anything else in rivers and seas that did not have fins and scales (Lev. 11:9-12). They could eat locusts, crickets, and grasshoppers, but no other insects (Lev. 11:20-23). Eating the wrong creatures, or even touching them, made a person unclean.

If a lizard fell in a pot and died, the pot became unclean, and anything prepared in that pot became unclean. The only right action would have been to break the pot (Lev. 11:29-35).

A woman was unclean for the entire time of her menstruation. Similarly, if a woman bore a male child, she was unclean for seven days, and had to go through a thirty-three-day time of purification before she could enter the sanctuary or touch anything considered holy. In the case of a female child, the period of uncleanness was extended to fourteen days and the time of purification to sixty-six days (Lev. 12:1-5). After the days of purifying, a woman was required to bring a one-year-old lamb to the priest for a burnt offering, plus a young pigeon or turtledove for a sin offering (Lev. 12:6).

A person with an eruption or spot on his or her skin was required to be examined by the priest. If the priest decided it was leprous, the person was pronounced unclean and subjected to the rules affecting lepers, to wit, wearing torn clothes, letting the hair hang loose about the head, covering the upper lip with the hand when others approached and crying, "Unclean, unclean," and dwelling alone in a habitation outside the camp or city (Lev. 13:1-46).

If it turned out that the person really didn't have leprosy, or if the leprosy abated, the rules for reinstatement in society said that the priest must examine the person outside the camp; two living birds must be provided; one would be killed in an earthen vessel over running water; the other bird would be dipped in the blood; the person to be cleansed would be sprinkled seven times in the blood, then pronounced clean; and the living bird would be released to fly away. Then the cleansed person would wash his or her clothes, shave off all his or her hair, bathe, and return to the camp. But even then he or she must dwell outside the camp for seven days before entering it (Lev. 14:1-9).

That was not all.

On the eighth day, the person was to take two male lambs and one ewe lamb, all without blemish, plus part of an ephah of fine flour mixed with oil, and an additional vessel of oil, to the priest, who would offer these gifts to the Lord for the inner cleansing of the person. In the process of this, the priest would pour some of the oil in his left hand, and with his right hand he would sprinkle some of it seven times before the Lord, then administer some to the tip of the right ear of the person being cleansed, and on the thumb of his right hand, and on the great toe of his right foot, and then put the rest of the oil on the person's head (Lev. 14:10-20).

Only then was the person considered completely cleansed.

Now, imagine, in the light of all of this, and much more besides, the shock wave that must have passed through Jesus' hearers when he said "Blessed are the pure in heart, for they will see God."

No red tape.

No mumbo jumbo.

No legal subtleties.

No codifications.

No intricate rituals to be performed.

Just purity of heart, and nothing else. God's anti-structure for the whole legal system. This alone was sufficient to get Jesus crucified in a nation run by scribes and Pharisees, for whom the legal system was life itself.

What does it mean to be "pure in heart"?

The Greek word for "pure" is *katharos*, which means clean, spotless, without blemish. In the Septuagint, the Greek version of the Old Testament, it appears more than 150 times, although most often in relation to the kind of ritual purification or cleansing mentioned above.

Some of the most significant references, however, are in the book of Job, in the portion where Job's so-called comforters argue with him about the calamities that have befallen him. Bildad the Shuhite tells Job that if he is "pure and upright" then God will surely rouse himself and hear Job's prayers (Job 8:6). Zophar the Naamathite repeats Job's own argument that his doctrine is pure and that he is "clean in God's sight" (Job. 11:4). Finally, Job himself says:

> My face is red with weeping,
>   and deep darkness is on my eyelids;
> though there is no violence in my hands,
>   and my prayer is pure.
>
> (Job 16:16-17)

Many scholars think that Job is one of the oldest books of the Old Testament, perhaps predating even the purification system of the Jews. If this is true, then the sense conveyed by the words *pure* and *clean* here is the more common one, without reference to ritual or ceremonial cleansing. It is the sense of being true, innocent, and without flaw. Bildad's linkage of *pure* and *upright* suggests a moral character akin to God's own, which is based on righteousness.

Another of the more telling references to purity and cleanness is in Psalm 24, which begins with the familiar words:

91

> The earth is the LORD's and all that is in it,
>   the world, and those who live in it. (v. 1)

Then the psalmist asks and answers an important question:

> Who shall ascend the hill of the LORD?
>   And who shall stand in his holy place?
> Those who have clean hands and pure hearts,
>   who do not lift up their souls to what is false,
>   and do not swear deceitfully. (vv. 3-4)

These people, says the psalmist, "will receive blessing from the LORD" (v. 5)—suggesting that Jesus may have had this very text in mind when he formulated the beatitude we are considering. If this is indeed the basis of the beatitude, then Jesus probably was thinking of persons who are innocent ("clean hands"), possessed of integrity ("do not lift up their souls to what is false"), and open in their dealings with God and other people ("do not swear deceitfully"). They are persons whose souls are transparent to God, genuinely sweet and good and trustworthy.

There are two kinds of purity among people I have known. One is a kind of natural purity, an almost genetic purity, that seems to characterize those who have it from the time they are children through the remainder of their lives. The other is an acquired purity, created either by some sudden transformation or by years of discipline and struggle to become good and righteous.

There is an example of natural purity in Fyodor Dostoyevsky's *The Brothers Karamazov*, in the young Alyosha Karamazov. Alyosha's father is a drunken, abusive man. One of his brothers is a wild, unpredictable *bon vivant*, a gambler, who spends his time carousing with women and ne'er-do-well friends. His other brother is a cynical intellectual, cold and rationalistic about everything. But Alyosha, for all of this, remains a simple, transparent man who turns a deaf ear to the crude language around him and reacts with unfailing compassion and kindness to everyone.

Dostoyevsky says: "Coming at twenty to his father's house, which was a very sink of filthy debauchery, he, chaste and pure as he was, simply withdrew into silence when to look on was unbearable, but without the slightest sign of contempt or condemnation" (*The Brothers Karamazov*, trans. Constance Garnett [New York: Modern Library, 1950], p. 17).

There was a woman in my parish in Virginia who had this inviolable sense of innocence and purity about her. Raised in a home with a stern, demanding father who believed girls inferior to boys and therefore openly preferred his son to her, she appeared nevertheless to develop no guile or animosity. When I knew them, the father had moved to a retirement home, and the daughter went to visit him every day, taking him books, flowers, candy, clothing, and other gifts on a regular basis. He remained harsh and unyielding, usually addressing her with scorn and abuse. Yet I never knew her to lose her sweet smile and pleasant composure. And, when her father became ill and bedridden, she cared for him with the diligence of a true saint, always exchanging gentleness and kindness for meanness and irascibility.

The secret of her gentleness, I am sure, was the natural chasteness of her soul. She loved flowers and trees and beautiful sunsets, and lived each day with a simple faith. She treated children especially with great tenderness, and made them feel special about themselves. There was nothing she would not do for anybody who needed it, and she brought joy into the lives of all who knew her. Her being was like clear honey, transparent to the goodness of God.

She was a woman of strong religious faith, to be sure, and this doubtless helped to shape the contours of her life. Yet there was something so consistently beautiful about her, so open and loving and radiant, that it seemed always to have been there. I have no doubt that if one could go back and visit her life at any point of her journey from the earliest years to the present, she would prove at all points to have been as pure and good as she is today.

I have never met John Leax, the poet, and yet I feel that he, too, is this kind of person. He and his family live on a small farm in upstate New York, which he operates in order to be near the natural world God has made, and he teaches creative writing at Houghton College. In his book of essays and memories *In Season and Out*, he has recorded the thoughts and activities of his life for an entire calendar year. In the entry for December 2, he speaks of the shortness of the days and how his outdoor tasks are finished except for bringing wood to the house. His thoughts are turning more and more to his students. He wants to write about them, to show how they enrich his life, and to discover the way his work with them is related to his work in the woods and garden.

The entry continues:

Early one afternoon before Thanksgiving I spent an hour talking to a fellow suffering from loneliness. Apart from allowing him to feel someone valued him enough to listen, I could do little for him. When I sat before my notebook that night, I wanted to get down my sense of helplessness before his plight; I wanted to get down the exhaustion and restoration I simultaneously experience in those situations. I wanted to say how giving brings unsought returns. But that night, caught up in the particular, I could not speak abstractly as I can tonight. Indeed, I did not want to. I left the student out of my entry altogether and wrote instead of hauling manure and the stewardship of the garden. Now as I write, the relationship between the two parts of the day is coming clear. My responsibility to my student and to my garden is the same responsibility. My caring for the earth, without ceasing to be important for its own sake, is an image of my caring for people. I learn one by doing the other. Wholeness will come to me when I cease to know them separately. (Grand Rapids: Zondervan Publishing House, 1985, p. 86)

These are the words of a good, gentle man, a man who is good by nature, not by design. He was undoubtedly a pleasure to his parents and is a gift to his wife, children, and students.

And what wonderful seasoning such people are in the general mixture of the population! Janwillem van de Wetering tells in his book *A Glimpse of Nothingness* about a Japanese film he saw once in Kyoto (he doesn't remember the name of the film) that opens on a ramshackle house in the slums of a large city. The owner of the house no longer cares about it, and some shady characters have taken it over. Two are burglars. Another is an invalid man who usually lies in the corner drunk while his wife goes out to beg. Another is a stuttering idiot, and yet another is an aging prostitute who has no more clients. They live in constant turmoil and argument.

One day an elderly Buddhist monk appears at the door and asks permission to enter, carrying with him only his bowl and a bell he sounds as he goes about begging. They think he may be an omen of luck, so allow him to take up residence with them. He sits in a corner of the room listening to them squabble about whose turn it is to sweep the floor. As soon as he understands what the fight is about, he gets up, takes the broom, and begins to sweep.

From this moment, the mood of the house changes. The inhabitants begin to assist one another. The burglars find an old blanket for the invalid. The prostitute becomes careful of her language. The invalid speaks kindly to the idiot and interferes when the burglars tease him.

The monk never criticizes or complains. He merely goes through the day being thoughtful and considerate. When the invalid is dying, he sits by his bed and holds his hand. When the old woman cries, he comforts her. When the idiot cannot find his flute, the monk finds it for him.

One day the burglars decide to stop burgling. They get honest jobs and use their first paycheck to buy food. They invite the monk to dinner. The prostitute changes her profession and becomes a charwoman.

The film ends with a party. It is New Year's Day, and the residents of the house decide to have a feast. After the meal, they join in making music. The idiot plays his flute and the others improvise instruments. The former burglars clap stones together and the former prostitute beats a chopstick against a bottle. Everybody sings. The song is delicate, sensitive, haunting. The monk strikes his handbell and the sound begins to vibrate. On this note, the film suddenly ends (*A Glimpse of Nothingness: Experiences in an American Zen Community* [New York: Ballantine Books, 1975], pp. 39-40).

Purity of heart is infectious. We are always aware of the way evil exerts its pernicious influence in a group or community. But sometimes we don't stop to think how much we owe to the truly good people who live among us. Their influence is felt too, often in quiet and unobtrusive ways. They challenge us to better and kinder living, and remind us, even unconsiously, of the presence of the deity in our midst.

No wonder Jesus said they will see the face of God.

But there is also, as I said, another kind of purity, the kind that is the result of either a sudden or a long-working transformation. We see it in the burglars and the prostitute of the story told by van de Wetering. Often, because of its contrast with the former behavior of a person, it is even more charming and compelling than natural purity.

Karl Menninger, in his now-classic psychological study *Man Against Himself*, tells about a woman brought to the Menninger Clinic in Topeka who was wild and erratic, had a terrible temper, and was given to uncontrollable outbursts. When not restrained, she performed unbelievable acts of aggression and hostility. Left alone in her room, she used the ordure from her bedpan to write obscene things on the walls. Eventually, through mental and chemical therapy, she was transformed into a person of gentleness and sensitivity. Menninger says it was an inspiration to enter her room and see her sitting quietly in bed, writing exquisitely beautiful poetry.

We think of a conversion like this as a miracle, and indeed it is.

The Bible is filled with stories of such miracles.

One of the most beautiful of these in the Old Testament is the story of David, after his adultery with Bathsheba and the birth of a child that died. Stricken with remorse, David wrote Psalm 51, one of the world's most beautiful hymns of repentance, begging for God to cleanse him of sin and restore him to purity. Indeed, the psalm is a running commentary on the meaning of purity of heart:

> Have mercy on me, O God,
>   according to your steadfast love;
> according to your abundant mercy
>   blot out my transgressions.
> Wash me thoroughly from my iniquity,
>   and cleanse me from my sin.
>
> . . . .
>
> You desire truth in the inward being;
>   therefore teach me wisdom in my secret heart.
> Purge me with hyssop, and I shall be clean;
>   wash me, and I shall be whiter than snow.
>
> . . . .

Create in me a clean heart, O God,
  and put a new and right spirit within me.
Do not cast me away from your presence,
  and do not take your holy spirit from me.
. . . .
O Lord, open my lips,
  and my mouth will declare your praise.
For you have no delight in sacrifice;
  if I were to give a burnt offering, you would not be pleased.
The sacrifice acceptable to God is a broken spirit;
  a broken and contrite heart, O God, you will not despise.
                                        (Psalm 51:1-2, 6-7, 10-11, 15-17)

The insights here are remarkable. David knows that if his heart is truly repentant, God can cleanse it of sin. He will be pure again, even whiter than snow. Then his whole spirit will be well. The usual sacrifices will avail nothing in a case like his. Only a broken and contrite heart will be acceptable to God.

It is but a step from this to the declaration of Jesus that God's real blessings are for the pure in heart, not those who laboriously and explicitly follow the letter of the Law in providing sacrifices and burnt offerings. In fact, Jesus may well have had this psalm as well as Psalm 24 in mind when he said "Blessed are the pure in heart, for they will see God." He was not assailing the Law and the system of sacrifices and offerings; he said he had come not to destroy the Law but to fulfill it. But he saw the ineffectiveness of sacrifice that did not represent the earnest desire of a person's heart, and at a stroke dismissed the structures of legalism for an emphasis on intention alone.

It was of course in Jesus himself that the entire system of atonement became localized and incarnate. From John the Baptist's cry at seeing him, "Behold the Lamb of God!," to his death on the cross as the sacrificial lamb *par excellence*, Jesus was the representative of God's rule, capable of forgiving sins and transforming people's lives. Wherever he went, his words, his touch, even his clothing, transmitted instant cleansing and acceptance from the Father. The Gerasene demoniac (Luke 8:26-33), the lame man at the pool of Bethzatha (John 5:1-9), the blind man near the pool of Siloam (John 9:1-12), the daughter of a Syrophoenician woman (Mark 7:24-30), and many others were instantly healed and transformed by the power of the coming reign.

The relationship between cleansing and healing is made very explicit in the story of the paralytic who was carried by four men and lowered through the roof of a house where Jesus was teaching. Seeing the faith of the men who carried the ill man, Jesus said to him, "Son, your sins are forgiven" (Mark 2:5). The scribes sitting there were immediately incensed, and demanded to know who gave him the power to forgive sins. To demonstrate that he had this power as the Son of man, the apocalyptic figure accompanying the reign of God, Jesus then commanded the man to take up his pallet and go home.

In Hebrew thought, any outward affliction was the sign of an inward deficiency. The person who was blind or deaf or lame or had leprosy was impure in heart, and the visible ailment or handicap merely proceeded from the more severe problem inside. The whole system of sacrifices for atonement was based on this. For Jesus to announce forgiveness, then, was the consummate sign of the arrival of the anti-structures. He brought in an instant the purification that the whole Jewish system had been striving for through centuries of careful discipline.

Thus baptism in the name of Jesus became a symbol of the washing away of sins. When Paul, addressing the mob that sought to kill him in Jerusalem, retold the narrative of his conversion, he said that Ananias came to him in Damascus and said, "And now why do you delay? Get up, be baptized, and have your sins washed away, calling on his [Jesus'] name" (Acts 22:16). There was never any doubt about where the power of this cleansing came from, as John in the book of Revelation makes clear: it is "from Jesus Christ, *the faithful witness, the First-born* from the dead, *the highest of earthly kings.* He loves us and has washed away our sins with his blood, and made us a *Kingdom of Priests* to serve his God and Father" (Rev. 1:5-6 NJB).

Later in the book of Revelation, when the writer sees a great crowd of people in white robes standing before the throne of the Lamb, he is told by one of the elders, "These are they who have come out of the great ordeal; they have washed their robes and made them white in the blood of the Lamb" (Rev. 7:14).

Inspired by imagery like this, many great sinners through the ages—people who were anything but pure before their encounter with Christ—have felt themselves purified by his blood and qualified to stand among those who shall see the face of God.

I recall an old roustabout who showed up one evening at the semi-rural church where I began my pastoral experience. He was a large, tough-looking man with tattoos on his arms, and eyes whose pupils had been permanently glazed by drugs and alcohol. He simply showed up as we were about to begin our evening service and said he had seen the lights in the church and thought he would like to worship with us. A ripple of apprehension passed through the people who were there. No one had ever seen him before. He looked dangerous and untrustworthy. What if he had a gun? Perhaps he had come to rob us. He sat on the back pew. Everyone in the room was visibly conscious of his being there through the entire service. People hurried home after the dismissal.

On Wednesday evening the man showed up again at prayer-meeting time. This time he was carrying a Bible. He said he had enjoyed the worship on Sunday evening and wanted to join us again. We felt more comfortable with him than we had before. After all, if he had intended to do us any harm, surely he would have done it on the first visit and disappeared from the community. I asked him if he would like to say a few words to the people who gathered that night. He said he would be happy to give his testimony.

Standing awkwardly before the little group, he clutched his Bible and looked at us. He had lived in many places and done many things, he said. Running away from home at fourteen, he had taken up with a gang of car thieves and dope addicts. His life had been wild and undisciplined, and he had drifted from one bad situation to another, spending time in prison on more than one occasion. He had been married twice and had grown children but didn't know where any of them were.

A fellow inmate in one of the prisons he had been in had been converted to Christ and read his Bible all the time. He had befriended this convert one day after he was in a fight, and the man had listened to the story of Jesus. Shortly after that, he had talked with the prison chaplain and given his heart to the Savior. For the first time since he was a small boy, he said, he knew what love was. He had vowed that when he got out of prison he was going to live a good life. He was traveling through the country looking for work. Now he read his Bible every day, and prayed as he walked through the countryside.

His Bible showed the wear. It appeared to have been handled a great deal.

That night a young couple in the church invited the man home with them to spend a few days while he was searching for work in the area. I was worried about what might happen, but they were people of faith and happy to be extending Christian hospitality. The man found a few days' work with a nearby farmer, so he lingered in the community until the following week. The couple seemed very happy to be entertaining him, and said he was good to help with chores around the house.

The next Sunday evening, when people were making song requests in the worship service, the man said he had a favorite hymn he would like us to sing. It was called "Nothing but the Blood." Our hymnals were of the folk variety, and the song was in them. I can still remember the beatific look on the man's face as he joined us in singing:

> What can wash away my sin?
> Nothing but the blood of Jesus.
> What can make me whole again?
> Nothing but the blood of Jesus.
>
> O precious is the flow
> that makes me white as snow;
> no other fount I know,
> nothing but the blood of Jesus.

I don't know what happened to the man. He wandered on after the few days' work was finished. But I shall always remember the ecstasy that showed in his whole being as he was singing that song. Whatever he had done, there was a kind of innocence or purity about him at that moment. Something had transformed him from the vile, offensive man he had been into a gentle, happy man who could be loved and trusted. It was the same power, I am convinced, that transforms all of us from creatures of darkness to children of the light.

The Apostle Paul best described this transformation in his letter to the Galatians, where he talked about what happens to us when the Spirit of God enters our lives. Before the Spirit comes in, he said, we live in the flesh—which was Paul's way of saying "in our own power." Our lives are then characterized by "fornication, impurity, licentiousness, idolatry, sorcery, enmities, strife, jealousy, anger, quarrels, dissensions, factions, envy, drunkenness, carousing, and things like these" (Gal. 5:19-21); that is, all the things we most dislike and hate in ourselves and others. But when the Spirit of God takes over, everything changes. Then we enjoy what Paul called "the fruit of the Spirit": "love, joy, peace, patience, kindness, generosity, faithfulness, gentleness, and self-control" (Gal. 5:22-23).

In short, we become pure in heart.

What did Jesus mean, the pure in heart will see God?

There is, to be sure, an apocalyptic dimension to what he intended. The saints in the book of Revelation, who have been washed in the blood of the Lamb, look on God directly. Their purity of heart enables them to perceive the holy, righteous One whose being is enthroned at the heart of the heavenly experience.

But suppose there is even more to this promise. Imagine that the pure in heart begin to have glimpses of God even in this life.

They do, don't they?

Haven't you ever noticed how, in those rare moments when you are feeling especially clean and good and exhilarated about life, you begin to sense a divine presence in everything? Oh, I don't mean anything pantheistic, that things around you actually become God. It is more subtle and beautiful than that. There is a kind of glory in everything, as if God were very near, as if it is God's presence that is actualizing everything, animating it, driving it, and causing it to pulsate with life and meaning.

That is the sensation produced by a pure heart.

I think of places in the writings of Annie Dillard and Marcus Bach and Virginia Stem Owens that seem to vibrate with their transparency to the holiness of God, as if through the childlike purity of their hearts they had seen something, had caught a fleeting glimpse, of the divine at play in our midst.

And Frederick Buechner, especially in his earlier books, was still writing truly and unselfconsciously because he had not yet become the darling of a coterie. This passage from *The Alphabet of Grace* has always made me shiver with excitement. Buechner wrote it on his birthday, a very rainy birthday. He gets up in the morning, does his ablutions, and then thinks about living the day as if it were the first of his life, "because," he says, "that is of course what it is."

It is your birthday, and there are many presents to open. The world is to open.

It rattles softly at the window like the fingers of a child as I sit on the edge of the tub to tie my shoes. It comes down the glass in crooked paths to stir my heart absurdly as it always has, and dear God in Heaven, the sound of it on the roof, on the taut black silk of the umbrella, on the catalpa leaves, dimpling the glassy surface of the peepering pond. It is the rain, and it tastes of silver; it is the rain, and it smells of christening. The rain is falling on the morning of my first day, and everything is wet with it: wet earth, wet fur, the smell of the grass when it is wet, the smell of the wet pavements of the city and the sound of tires on the wet streets, the wet hair and face of a woman doing errands in the rain. Wherever my feet take me now, it will be to something wet, something new, that I have never seen before.

You wonder about life on distant worlds if there is any life on them, the extravagances of nature there, the convolutions of unimaginable histories and geographies there, and now on this distant world that is yours and that you have awakened to, you will see it all for yourself. You have only to look through this rain-washed glass to see what astronomers from other worlds would travel light-years to see: this third planet from the sun with the rain falling, the glint of water taps, tub rim, through the window the cat licking its silken wrist under the eaves. The curious rendezvous as you get to your feet, both shoes tied, and stand there with the whole weight of you, everything that goes by your name, pressing down for all you're worth upon the shaggy pelt of this planet which with its whole vast bulk and for all its worth presses up to resist you—this encounter, this tryst, between you and your planet, each of you so gentle yet unyielding and firm with the other. And you will see faces before this first day is done: each the only one of its kind in the universe, each the face of a high king whose line reaches back unbroken through unnumbered generations, through ancient cities and forgotten battles, past dim, gibbering rain forests to the very beginnings of history itself and beyond, and they will speak to you in words soft and worn from centuries of handling, will say A, B and C to you, E and F and G and H, and will say O to you, O, O, high king to high king as you meet in the mystery of this rainy morning while the cat buries her mess by the broken red wagon and leaves the color of sunrise fall out of the sky. (Frederick Buechner, *The Alphabet of Grace* [New York: Seabury Press, 1970], pp. 36-38)

Do you see what I mean? Transparency. God just the other side of everything. Holiness brimming at the edge of our consciousness. Caught like a snapshot, an instantly fading snapshot, by the momentary purity of the heart.

And if this is only a hint, a small prelude to what heaven will be, yes, the pure in heart will be blessed indeed, for their hearts will flutter for eternity at the vision of God. The joy is almost unbearable.

CHAPTER SEVEN

BLESSED ARE THE PEACEMAKERS

Blessed are the peacemakers, for they will be called children of God" (Matt. 5:9).

Eirenopoios is the Greek word. "Shapers" or "crafters" or "makers" of peace. It is a unique word. This is the only time it appears in the Scriptures.

Who are they, the peacemakers? Which of the following would you see as qualifying?

Soldiers
Doctors
Lawyers
Teachers
Telephone operators
Referees
Labor negotiators
Ecologists
Counselors
Farmers
Artists

If you said soldiers, lawyers, referees, labor negotiators, and counselors, you gave the traditional answers. These are indeed professions accustomed to dealing with conflict, ironing out disputes, and enforcing decisions.

But such an answer tends to address the *negative* side of peacemaking, while the Bible sees it in a much more *positive* light. The

Jewish understanding of *shalom* (the Hebrew word for "peace") was a great deal broader than the mere absence of conflict. It meant favor and fullness and richness and joy, all at the same time. Its common picture was of a man and his wife and their children on a plot of ground that belonged to them, living in harmony with their neighbors, with their own personal fig tree and sheep and goats, with a never-failing spring of water, and a good relationship with God. It was a combination of soil and atmosphere and nutrients in which the essence of being human could achieve its highest levels, fulfilling what the Creator intended his children to become.

Johannes Pedersen, in his monumental *Israel: Its Life and Culture,* said that peace, for the Jew, could not be understood apart from community. When there is harmony in the community and the entire community is penetrated by a sense of the blessing of God, then there is true peace.

> Its fundamental meaning is totality; it means the untrammelled, free growth of the soul. But this, in its turn, means the same as harmonious community; the soul can only expand in conjunction with other souls. There is "totality" in a community when there is harmony, and the blessing flows freely among its members, everyone giving and taking whatever he is able to. (London: Oxford University Press, 1959, vol. I, pp. 263-64)

Thus the doctors, teachers, telephone operators, ecologists, farmers, and artists are also essential to peacemaking, for they often do even more than soldiers, lawyers, and negotiators to bring harmony and blessing to a community. They provide the kind of vision and service necessary to wholeness of life, and thus give depth and fulfillment to the very concept of peace or *shalom.*

There is a beautiful passage in Leviticus, one of the books of the Torah, that describes the kind of peace or fullness God wants for his people. It says:

> If you follow my statutes and keep my commandments and observe them faithfully, I will give you your rains in their season, and the land shall yield its produce, and the trees of the field shall yield their fruit. Your threshing shall overtake the vintage, and the vintage shall overtake the sowing; you shall eat your bread to

the full, and live securely in your land. And I will grant peace in the land, and you shall lie down, and no one shall make you afraid; I will remove dangerous animals from the land, and no sword shall go through your land. You shall give chase to your enemies, and they shall fall before you by the sword. Five of you shall give chase to a hundred, and a hundred of you shall give chase to ten thousand; your enemies shall fall before you by the sword. I will look with favor upon you and make you fruitful and multiply you; and I will maintain my covenant with you. You shall eat old grain long stored, and you shall have to clear out the old to make way for the new. I will place my dwelling in your midst, and I shall not abhor you. And I will walk among you, and will be your God, and you shall be my people. I am the LORD your God, who brought you out of the land of Egypt, to be their slaves no more; I have broken the bars of your yoke and made you walk erect. (Lev. 26:3-13)

The emphasis on warfare is not what it appears. It is not meant as sword-rattling bloodthirstiness, but as joy in true security that is able to fend off invaders with an ease never known among the ancient peoples. The picture is one of harmony, blessedness, full-ness. Those who had been slaves in Egypt were now free, and not only free but gifted with luxuriating in a land that produced plentifully, so that one harvest extended into another and there was no want at any time. And the sense of communion included not only families and tribes but God as well, dwelling in their midst and tending to their needs.

This was the high vision of *shalom*—of true peace—the Jews never lost. It was not absence of fighting. It was strength, whole-ness, well-being. It was richness, plenitude, joy. It was, in a sense, the anti-structures, the reign of God that never came because they sinned and broke the commandments and forgot that Yahweh was their deity.

This is why the Messiah was identified in prophecy as "Won-derful Counselor, Mighty God, Everlasting Father, Prince of Peace" (Isa. 9:6). His coming would bring to fulfillment a promise never before actually realized, because the willfulness of Israel had prevented it centuries before.

The Gospel writers were quick to recognize a connection between the coming of Jesus and the ancient promises to Israel.

When Zechariah, the father of John the Baptist, was filled with the Holy Spirit and allowed to speak, he predicted that the child to be born of Mary would "give light to those who sit in darkness and in the shadow of death" and guide their feet "into the way of peace" (Luke 1:79). The angels who appeared to the shepherds announced

"Glory to God in the highest heaven,
and on earth peace among those whom he favors!"
(Luke 2:14)

When Jesus was anointed by a sinful woman at the home of Simon the Pharisee, he defended her against the remonstrations of his host and said to her, "Your faith has saved you; go in peace" (Luke 7:50). When a woman with an unquenchable flow of blood (who would therefore by Jewish law have dwelled in a continual state of uncleanness) touched him and was healed, Jesus said to her, "Daughter, your faith has made you well; go in peace" (Luke 8:48). As Jesus was taking leave of his disciples at the Last Supper, he said to them, "Peace I leave with you; my peace I give to you. I do not give to you as the world gives" (John 14:27). His last words to them in that long final discourse were: "I have said this to you, so that in me you may have peace. In the world you face persecution. But take courage; I have conquered the world!" (John 16:33). And his first words to them after the Resurrection, repeated three times in the space of only eight verses, were "Peace be with you" (John 20:19-26).

The words *Peace be with you* (*shalom aleichem*) were, of course, a customary Jewish greeting. But for the early Christians they obviously took on a special meaning when spoken by Jesus. He was the bearer of this peace, the guarantor of the rule of God that would usher in the age of eternal peace.

Not everyone, in this interim age, would experience the peace of God. In fact, some would experience exactly the opposite. "Do not think that I have come to bring peace to the earth," Jesus said on one occasion; "I have not come to bring peace, but a sword" (Matt. 10:34; see also Luke 12:49-53). He saw the world being divided in its loyalties by his coming. Even within single households, sons would be set against fathers and daughters against mothers. But he viewed this as part of the universal conflict that must precede the golden time of peace.

What the Prince of Peace intended by announcing the blessedness of peacemakers, then, was a commendation of all those who live by the vision of God's peaceful rule (what artist Edward Hicks called "the peaceable kingdom") and live or act in any way to further that rule. Such persons may be ecologists, teachers, writers, ministers, nursery workers, social workers, committed legislators, doctors, nurses, missionaries, researchers, or philanthropists. They may also be soldiers, lawyers, merchants, and labor negotiators, provided that they are persons devoted to human welfare and the ideals of God's reign. The important thing is that they aim at enriching life and its environment for others and do not seek merely to do their jobs for personal reasons.

Peacemaking can be a highly individualistic endeavor. When I think of peacemakers I have known or heard about, I think of such diverse persons as Mother Teresa, Jonas Salk, Jimmy Carter, Martin Luther King, Jr., Bob Hope, Anwar Sadat, Bishop Tutu, Mikhail Gorbachev, Henri Nouwen, Barbara Bush, Ralph Nader, and James Baker. Each has made invaluable contributions to the struggle for human wholeness in a broken world.

I also think of a Kentucky farmer who used to come through the retirement home where my father was living, distributing apples and candy to the old folks. This farmer was like a gentle ray of sunshine breaking into the gloom of the hallways and rooms of the home, always smiling and speaking cheerily and smelling of the fresh fields from which he had come. I asked if he had a relative in the home and he said no, he had once come to visit someone there and had brought some apples from his orchard, which everybody seemed to enjoy, so he had just continued to come over the years. "At Christmas I play Santie for them," he said, "and hand out candy and chewing gum. They always seem to get a kick out of it." He was not a wealthy man by the world's standards—far from it—but he was immensely wealthy in the kingdom of God.

And I think of a doctor's wife and her strawberry pies. This woman had several baskets of strawberries she was afraid were going to ruin. So she spent Sunday afternoon making pies of them. Her husband asked her why she was doing it. "Oh," she said, "the Lord will give us somebody to help us eat them." That night at her church she went around inviting people to come over to her house for pie and ice cream after the service. She saw one rather lonely looking woman whom she didn't know and, acting on instinct, went up and invited her, too. After the pie and ice cream, they were all sitting around the living room talking when the woman suddenly burst into tears.

"I'm sorry," she said when she had regained her composure. "I was just so happy I couldn't help it." She explained that she had been through some very difficult times. Her husband had deserted her with four small children, and her life had been very hard of late. She had come to church that evening hoping to find friendship. "I prayed all day that God would give me some new friends," she said, smiling through her tears, "and now here you are!"

This woman was being a peacemaker with her strawberries. She made the world more whole that night for a woman who was lonely, and probably for everyone else who was there as well.

And I think, too, of an Air Force colonel in charge of the chaplains in the Pacific. I met the colonel several years ago when I was leading workshops for chaplains in Japan, Thailand, and the Philippines. He told me his dream one day as we were strolling through Chiangmai, Thailand, looking at Buddhist temples. The colonel was from Sneedville, Tennessee, the county seat of Hancock County, the poorest district in the entire Appalachian region. According to U.S. records, there were fewer than 350 paying jobs in the entire county. The colonel had been collecting antique furniture all over the Orient, wherever his work took him. He was especially fond of clocks. What he wanted to do when he retired from the Air Force, he said, was return to Hancock County, build a furniture factory that would reproduce these antiques, and end the unemployment problem of the people among whom he had grown up.

A few years after that, I heard that he had retired and returned to Hancock County. One day my wife and I drove over to Sneedville to see him. As we crossed the county line, we saw fifty or sixty cars parked alongside the road, apparently where people carpooling to jobs in other counties had left them for the day. The colonel was happy to see us. He could hardly wait to take us by the site where his furniture factory was being readied. Then he took us by another site and said he had not been content to build a single factory; a second was going to go up on this additional site.

I have not seen him since that day. But I have heard from friends that the factories were completed and put into operation and were phenomenally successful from the beginning. They weren't sure that he was getting rich, they said, for they had an idea that he was plowing back most of his profits into plans to further help his community and county. But they knew he was supremely happy.

He should have been, because he was living the role of a peacemaker. He was helping to shape the peace of God for the people in his hometown. In his career, he had roamed the world. But in the end he was happy to return to his roots and do what he could to make life richer and fuller for others.

Such people, said Jesus, "will be called children of God." The sons and daughters of the Great One, the One who desires peace and fullness in all the world.

It is a beautiful designation.

There is a sign on an old barn just outside Broadway, in the English Cotswolds—or there is if it hasn't completely faded out by now. I saw it three or four years ago as I was walking through the rain and stopped to look at the peaceful farmyard scene. It said, Bellow & Son, Ltd., Makers—Leominster.

It didn't say what Bellow and his son made—only that they were makers.

I have often thought about that sign and what it boded for Bellow and his son. What a wonderful age it must have been, when sons became part of their fathers' businesses and eventually became the managers and took their own sons into partnership. How proud both Mr. Bellow and his son must have been when that sign was painted there, announcing their working relationship.

And how glorious it is for us to be called the children of the Creator of the world, just because we desire the fullness of the creation and are willing to invest our lives in helping to achieve that fullness.

It should give a lift to our steps today.

Just imagine: God and Son, Makers; or God and Daughter, Makers. It's a beautiful thought, isn't it?

CHAPTER EIGHT

BLESSED ARE THE PERSECUTED

Blessed are those who are persecuted for righteousness' sake, for theirs is the kingdom of heaven" (Matt. 5:10).

This is the last of the Beatitudes. Matthew has Jesus expanding on it and making it much more personal, shifting from the third-person to the second-person pronoun, to make a transition between the Beatitudes and the other thoughts that will follow. Here is the expansion: "Blessed are you when people revile you and persecute you and utter all kinds of evil against you falsely on my account. Rejoice and be glad, for your reward is great in heaven, for in the same way they persecuted the prophets who were before you" (Matt. 5:11-12). This added saying is a little like the device of parallelism in the Psalms; it basically repeats the idea of the beatitude, but with a slight enhancement.

Together, the thoughts demonstrate a strong sense of realism. The first seven beatitudes describe the kinds of persons who will be taken care of in the reign of God, who will suddenly find themselves "in" instead of "out" in society, "up" instead of "down." God's justice and mercy will perform this drastic inversion on the world, and the prostitutes, tax-collectors, crippled people, and beggars will find themselves unexpectedly elevated above the rich, self-righteous people who sought to fashion heaven according to their own ideals. The Lazaruses will look down from the bosom of Abraham and see the wealthy landowners suffering in hell. But Jesus knows that the rich, ruling class—the movers and shapers of society—will not accept this inversion lying down. They will oppose it with every fiber

113

of their beings and will come down with force on anyone who preaches such a reversal of fortunes. Thus the final, or perhaps additional, beatitude (seven was usually the number representing fullness, and this one makes eight) is about all those who will suffer in behalf of the new rule of God as it takes effect. It is directed at anyone who stands for the righteousness of God, who is counted on the side of the kingdom and is persecuted for it.

It was altogether an appropriate concluding beatitude, because righteousness inevitably involves suffering. Jesus himself was the example *par excellence.* He was the best and wisest man who ever lived, and yet he endured the cruelest, most humiliating death his times could offer, not because he only happened to get caught crosswise in the political situation of his day but precisely because his closeness to God directly exposed him to the hatred and villainy of the enemies of God. Jesus knew, and warned his disciples, that it would always be thus, with them as well as himself.

"If the world hates you," he said,

> "be aware that it hated me before it hated you. If you belonged to the world, the world would love you as its own. Because you do not belong to the world, but I have chosen you out of the world—therefore the world hates you. Remember the word that I said to you, 'Servants are not greater than their master.' If they persecuted me, they will persecute you." (John 15:18-20)

The three Synoptic Gospels and the Gospel of Thomas all carry the parable Jesus told about the vineyard owner who sent his servants to collect some of the benefits of the vineyard. They were beaten and turned away. Then the owner sent his son, thinking the tenants would respect him. But the tenants, seeing the son as the only person standing between them and ownership of the vineyard, killed the son (Matt. 21:33-42; Mark 12:1-11; Luke 20:9-18; Gos. Thom. 65-66). In each case, the story comes after Jesus' entry into Jerusalem, shortly before the crucifixion. It is seen, in other words, as an interpretation of what Jesus has experienced in Israel; he has come to God's favorite vineyard to enter the Owner's claim on it and has experienced rejection from the spurious managers who have taken it over. The only further step is to be his actual death at the hands of the evil ones occupying his Father's property.

In this world where evil has risen up to contest the good, where the weeds quickly spring up to choke out the wheat, the struggle for good is never easy. It will always be met with treachery, deceit, betrayal, and open warfare. Those who occupy the places of power and control will never surrender them without force. They will use their positions to quash and obliterate all opposition. Those who are good, gentle, and righteous will always be at a tactical disadvantage when dealing with sleazy, mean, selfish, and unrighteous people, for the righteous will try to play fair while the others do not. Taught to behave honestly and forthrightly in all things, they will usually find themselves outmaneuvered by persons eager to win at all costs.

It would be easy enough to write the history of vital Christianity as a history of the persecution of Christians. As Herbert Workman says in his book *Persecution in the Early Church*, there would probably have been no persecution if the church had not been aggressive in following the mandate of its Lord to preach the gospel everywhere. "A Christianity which had ceased to be aggressive would speedily have ceased to exist" (Oxford: Oxford University Press, 1980, p. 20).

The church's faithfulness to Christ first brought it under fire from the Jews, who were in an unusually tense situation with the Romans to begin with. There were many zealous groups of Jews who believed they must rid their homeland of the hated occupation forces before the Messiah would come, and rumors of sedition and revolution were therefore rife throughout the first century. It was the charge of treason brought against Jesus that made it impossible for Pilate not to deal personally with his case and eventually hand him over to the soldiers for crucifixion. Similarly, in the cases of Paul and other apostles, the delicacy of Jewish relations with Rome often led to imprisonment or martyrdom for offenses that might have been less noticeable in other times.

Jewish opponents often fed the flames of rumor and ridicule in other lands, and Christians became commonly suspected of immorality, illegal activities, and inhuman practices. Because

115

they met privately and in secret, they were accused of every-thing from having orgies to plotting to overthrow the govern-ment. It was even said that they sacrificed their own children to appease their God, and consumed their flesh and blood in the communion services. In general, they were regarded as ignorant, superstitious fools, nuisances, and threats to the order and decency of the empire. And, because they refused to surrender to the polytheistic structures of Roman religion and to take an oath to the emperor as a god, they were considered both *atheos,* or atheistic, and treasonous.

How thoroughly and grievously they were persecuted depended on local circumstances. It appears that magistrates and rulers were given wide discretion in enforcing laws, with a general authority known as *coercitio,* or power of coercion, and there was considerable unevenness in the way they applied this authority. We know there were certain periods—such as the one following the great fire in Rome in A.D. 64, which Nero blamed on the Christians—when persecution became much more intense and widespread than at other times. But Christians who got in trouble for any reason were much more at risk, given their gen-eral reputation, than most other citizens of the empire. (For an excellent account of the legal aspects of persecution in this era, see Leon Hardy Canfield, *The Early Persecutions of the Christians* [New York: AMS Press, 1968].)

There are horrible stories of the indignities and atrocities suf-fered by Christians in the centuries before Constantine made Christianity a legal religion, and then the religion of the empire, in the early fourth century. In various times and places, they were stripped naked and beaten in public arenas; lowered into vats of boiling oil; blinded by having their eyes seared or pulled out; deafened by having hot coals placed in their ears; branded by red-hot irons; separated from limbs, breasts, or genitals; hung and beaten until their bowels gushed forth; nailed to crosses; rectally impaled on sharp wooden posts; mauled by wild animals; gored on the horns of bulls; dragged over beds of nails or sharpened sea shells; tied in bags and low-ered under water until they drowned; and pulled apart by horses.

It is hardly to be wondered at, under the circumstances, that

116

apostasy or falling away from the faith was a central problem in the early church. Easily half the literature in the New Testament was originally written in the attempt to staunch the flow of members from the highly vulnerable little congregations of the first century. Yet Tertullian could declare that the blood of the martyrs is the seed of the church (*Apologetics*, 50) and Clement of Rome saw in the phoenix, the mythological bird that died and was resurrected every 500 years, a sign of Christian endurance (*Epistle to the Corinthians*, xxv-xxvi).

Imprisonment and martyrdom were of course not the only ways in which the early Christians suffered. Many faced subtler forms of discomfort or discrimination. It is clear even from the literature of the New Testament that following Christ posed difficulties in the home, in society, and in the marketplace. Marriages were often strained by a husband or wife becoming a Christian while the other remained an unbeliever. Families were known to expel members who claimed allegiance to Christ. Christians found it difficult to attend banquets or celebrations held in the temples of pagan gods, where the food was usually offered to the gods before being set before the guests. Carpenters, masons, and other craftsmen among the faithful found themselves unable to work on heathen shrines or replicate images of gods and goddesses. For all of Christianity's emphasis on the grace of God, a strong works-righteousness prevailed among the Christian fellowships, creating divisions between devoted Christians and much of the pagan society around them.

Persecution of the faithful did not entirely cease after the legalization of Christianity. The history of the Middle Ages is replete with stories of atrocities suffered by Christians at the hands of infidels, particularly the Muslims. Christian missionaries often met with hardship and death under various regimes and at various times in Africa and Asia. And there is now considerable literature about the persecution of the saints under modern communism. A law passed in the Soviet Union in 1929 forbade Christians to openly profess their faith. Worship services were severely restricted. Thousands of Christian pastors were deported to Siberia. Of the more than 70,000 Russian Orthodox churches in existence in 1917, only about 500 remained in 1939 (Winrich Scheffbuch, *Christians Under the Hammer and Sickle*, trans.

Mark A. Noll [Grand Rapids: Zondervan Publishing House, 1974], p. 16). In satellite countries such as Czechoslovakia and Romania, pastors, active lay members, and their families were often imprisoned and their goods impounded. The goal of the Communist Party was the complete extinction of Christianity within its member nations and eventually in the entire world.

Among those who suffered for Christ under this policy of discrimination and persecution were the Romanian Jewish Christians Richard and Sabina Wurmbrand, whom I have mentioned earlier in this book. Sabina later wrote the book *The Pastor's Wife*, in which she told of their experiences with "a Christianity that meant sacrifice and self-renunciation" (London: Hodder & Stoughton, 1970, p. 69). Romania had survived the horrors of Nazism in World War II, only to fall under the domination of Moscow when the war ended. In 1947 the arrests began. Rigged elections gave the Communists absolute control of the country. One Sunday morning in late February, 1948, Richard Wurmbrand walked alone to church; he never arrived. Sabina later learned that he had been arrested as a "political" prisoner. She was not allowed to visit with him. Her ration card was taken away, because families of political prisoners were not allowed ration cards. Without a ration card, she could not get a job because people without ration cards theoretically did not exist.

"How am I to live?" she asked the authorities. "And my son?"

"That's your business," they replied (*The Pastor's Wife*, p. 33).

Her son, Mahai, went to stay with friends in the country. Sabina continued to work secretly for the church, visiting the sick in the disguise of a nurse or a charwoman. Then, at 5:00 one morning in August, there was a pounding on her door. The police crashed in and began tearing the house apart, pretending to look for hidden arms. Finding none, they arrested her and threw her into a room with hundreds of other "undesirable" women. She was to spend years in Jilava prison, working at hard labor, receiving scant food and medical care, having insufficient clothing for the cold, winter months, and sleeping at night in a crowded barracks. It was cause for celebration, she said, when the women found three beans in their soup instead of two. Only one time, in all the years of her incarceration, was she permitted to see her son Mihai, and then only for fifteen minutes across an intervening space of ten yards, with the guards standing beside them to hear anything that was said. The fifteen minutes flew by as they stood gazing upon each other, saying little. At last, before they parted, Sabina shouted to him, "Mihai, believe in Jesus with all your heart!" (*The Pastor's Wife*, p. 89).

The years in prison had not dulled her strong faith or commitment to her Lord.

One of the tragic notes in the history of religious persecution is the way devout Christians have often come under attack from other Christians. The more Christianity became entrenched as the accepted religion of an area, developing strong traditions and rigid hierarchies within the local or regional society, the more pressure individual Christians began to suffer from their own official judicatories. The annals of the church are filled with disgraceful episodes in which believers endured persecution, imprisonment, and even death because they disagreed in faith or practice with fellow Christians. The religious wars of the sixteenth, seventeenth, and eighteenth centuries resulted in the deaths of thousands of devoted followers of Christ, and the strife in modern Ireland, drawn along Protestant-Catholic lines, is ample proof that such terrible and ironic warfare among the so-called faithful is far from over.

Many Christians in North America seem hardly aware of the great suffering today of fellow Christians in Central and South America, where reform efforts within the Roman Catholic Church and the local governments have met with stout resistance from traditionalist clerics and other persons in high places. Reform efforts intensified after 1968, when the general assembly of Latin American bishops met in Medellin, Colombia, and many bishops, priests, and members of local congregations began actively siding with the poor, exploited natives of their lands. It has been estimated that between 1968 and 1979, when the general assembly met again in Puebla, more than 1,500 Christians were imprisoned, exiled, tortured, or murdered in Paraguay and Bolivia alone because they adopted the cause of the *campesinos*, or people with little or no land, against the *caciques*, or village bosses, and the large landowners, nonreforming bishops, and regional dictators.

A document circulated in 1975 among the "higher echelons

of the Bolivian church" advised special tactics in dealing with progressive Christians. Among these tactics were: isolating progressive leaders and bringing them into conflict with the indigenous clergy; keeping close watch on certain religious orders, such as the Dominicans, Oblates, and Jesuits; cooperating with the CIA in order to obtain information about certain priests and their friends in North America; watching the houses of suspected priests and bishops to be sure they do not conceal "dangerous" clerics; bringing apprehended suspects to secret rendezvous and informing the bishops only after arrests are *faits accomplis*; inserting among the personal effects of arrested persons subversive propaganda material or weapons, preferably high-caliber pistols; publishing false reports in newspapers and on television harming the reputations of progressive leaders; publicly cultivating relations with indigenous priests in order to avert the impression of a general persecution; and assuring agents of misconduct a share of the confiscated property of affected priests and other Christians (Martin Lange and Reinhold Iblacker, *Witnesses of Hope: The Persecution of Christians in Latin America* [Maryknoll, N.Y.: Orbis Books, 1981], pp. 14-16).

One of the heroic tales of committed believers in Latin America is that of Dr. Sheila Cassidy, a British-trained medical doctor who assumed the directorship of a clinic for the poor in El Salto, one of the most miserable slums of Santiago, Chile. Becoming friends with many of the priests and sisters who worked in the slums, she was called by a priest one night to give first aid to a leftist revolutionary with two gunshot wounds in his leg. The aid was administered in a nuns' cloister, and the man was later removed to the residence of a papal delegate.

Ten nights later, Dr. Cassidy went to the house of a missionary society where she was attending to an American nun who had suffered a breakdown from overwork. While she was there, the house was surrounded and shots rang out. She was arrested and taken to one of the centers of the secret police, where she was three times subjected to electrical torture, at least once with a movable electrode in her vagina, until she confessed to having treated the revolutionary and led the police to the building where she had done it. She was held in strict isolation for two more months, and afterward released because of diplomatic efforts.

Forced to leave Chile, Dr. Cassidy returned to England, where she became a novice in a convent of Benedictine nuns. Reflecting on her torture, she said:

> I remember the time when I was lying naked on the bed, with my arms and legs stretched out, and I was tortured mercilessly. I had the impression that I was present at the passion of Jesus more as a participant than as an onlooker. It was not the feeling one has when meditating on the sufferings of Christ, when one is a bystander, seeing someone else suffering and having deep sympathy for that person. Mine was a very clear impression that *I* was *there*, suffering with Christ and no longer merely as an onlooker. (Quoted in Lange and Iblacker, *Witnesses of Hope*, p. 104)

Does all of this sound foreign and strange? Perhaps it is because it emanates from the Third World, where dictatorships still exist and the power structures have not been altered to agree with modern standards. Once the process of democratization has achieved its universal ends, things will surely be much better. Then laws will protect those with Christian intentions and persecution will cease.

Look at our own country, which was built on Christian principles. Here, people are not ill-treated for espousing the cause of Christ and wanting to do the right thing.

Sounds good, doesn't it?

But what is the reality?

Even here in nominally Christian America, people suffer for spiritual or religious commitment.

Think of Martin Luther King, Jr., and other martyrs who died for the cause of racial justice.

Recall the many persons who were watched, imprisoned, and otherwise persecuted by the government for their conscientious objection to American involvement in the war in Vietnam.

Reflect on the hundreds of people presently kept under surveillance, hassled, restricted, and imprisoned because they have taken part in the Christian sanctuary movement, giving aid and shelter to refugees from oppressive governments in Central and South America.

One night at dinner in a United Methodist conference in Arizona, I sat by a lovely young woman who had felt led through prayer, Bible study, and reflection to participate in this movement by working to care for refugees in her local church. She was only twenty-two years old. Yet she had been arrested by the FBI, held in prison, warned to discontinue her "anti-American" activities, and told, after her release, that she would be sent to prison for an indeterminate number of years if she crossed the borders of her state. A graduate student in medical school, she had planned to complete her studies in another state. Because of her commitment to the gospel of Christ, she has had to abandon her plans and live in Arizona for the remainder of her life.

I was living in Virginia when newspapers carried accounts of Dr. Elisabeth Kübler-Ross's intentions to build a hospice in a nearby county for children with AIDS. She had made a considerable amount of money both as a doctor and as the author of several best-selling books about death and dying. Now she wanted to give back to the public some of the proceeds of her illustrious career by building this center. At first, she was publicly praised for this charitable act. Then complaints from "concerned neighbors," many as far as fifty miles away, began to circulate about the risk factor to those who had never been exposed to the AIDS virus. What if the wind carried germs to others in the area, exposing them to the dreaded disease? There were cross-burnings, lawsuits, letters to the editor, a veritable concert of recriminations and vilifications. Workers refused to work on the project. Planners withdrew support. Dr. Kübler-Ross had to forgo her dream of helping the children. Many nominally Christian people rejoiced, often implying, if they did not say it outright, that AIDS is a judgment sent by God and should not be contravened by a hospice for anyone affected by the virus.

A retired minister was invited to plan a series of Lenten breakfasts in a church in California. He thought it was time for the church to stop having its usual course of bland meditations on Christian character or the spiritual life and face squarely up to its calling as a witness for peace and justice in the world. Accordingly, he planned a series of programs on such topics as drugs, poverty, homelessness, illiteracy, AIDS, and racial equality. He secured Dr. John Bennett, retired president of Union Theological Seminary in New York and a renowned ethicist, as the introductory speaker, and similarly qualified men and women, some of whom were from minorities, to lead the subsequent discussions.

It was, in my opinion, an outstanding series, capable of provoking great thought and enlarging Christian sensibilities about areas of the church's common life that require constant review and action. But reaction from traditionalists was swift and well defined. This was Lent, when they were accustomed to meditating on the sufferings of their Lord. They did not like to be reminded of the negative state of their environment, which they got quite enough of from television and the newspapers. They attended church and supported mission enterprises in other parts of the world; why should they be expected to address matters of such local and immediate concern? Who was this retired minister, anyway? He was a troublemaker who had moved to California from another state a few years ago. As far as most of them were concerned, he could go back where he had come from. They never wanted to have another program of this kind in their church.

The next year, the leaders of the congregation mandated a return to the usual Lenten fare. When the retired minister continued to attend the church and was accidentally given a part in a retreat program, two ministers on the church staff took it upon themselves to confront him about his "disruptive influence" and invited him to leave the congregation. Deeply hurt, he stayed away from church for several weeks. Only one person called to ask about him. Most people merely wrote him off as a radical and said the church was better off without him. Now wounded beyond repair, he vowed never to attend the church again and has since moved to another state.

It happens virtually all the time and in every place. People who are strongly committed to virtue, goodness, value, justice, and compassion constantly set themselves up for confrontation and embarrassment, if not outright persecution and ostracism. Think of them—those who take the side of the poor and homeless; those who try to establish halfway houses for reformed prisoners; those who join the fight against pollution and the despoiling of the planet; those who contend for more ethical politics; those who work for fairness in school issues; those who befriend homosexuals; those who try to improve race relations; those who seek ecumenical relations among the churches and with people of other faiths; those who oppose unfair labor laws or go up against management in behalf of workers; those who campaign for better conditions for the elderly; those who expose corruption in government or industry; those who refuse to support unjust wars with their taxes; those who speak out against sub-Christian attitudes or practices within their own congregations. The list could go on and on. The point is, Jesus was right about persecution for righteousness' sake. It is bound to come to all who are genuinely faithful to his vision of the kingdom.

Yet these people are deeply blessed, said Jesus, for in the anti-structures, when the rule of God has fully come, they will be the ones at the center of the kingdom. Evil will be banished to the lake of fire; unrighteousness will be purged and fully dealt with; and only what is true and good and holy will remain.

And perhaps you have noticed this about Jesus' statement: the blessedness of which he spoke is present tense.

It is not happiness in some future time.

It is happiness now.

How can this be?

Surely it has something to do with the nature of the reign that is coming, and how the vision of it sustains Christ's true followers even before it has fully arrived. Like the great saints described in the book of Hebrews, they look forward to a "well-founded city, designed and built by God" (Heb. 11:10, NJB), and the mere thought of it is enough to keep them going when the way is stony and beset by problems.

The writer of Hebrews found great consolation in the fact that Jesus walked this way before us. Concluding his lengthy catalog of references to the many prophets, leaders, and common folks who have also preceded us, some of whom "were sawn in two," "killed by the sword," "went about in skins of sheep and goats, destitute, persecuted, tormented," "wandered in deserts and mountains, and in caves and holes in the ground" (Heb. 11:37-38), the writer of Hebrews reached his crescendo by alluding to the Master himself.

> Therefore, since we are surrounded by so great a cloud of witnesses, let us also lay aside every weight and the sin that clings so closely, and let us run with perseverance the race that is set before us, looking to Jesus the pioneer and perfecter of our faith, who for the sake of the joy that was set before him endured the cross, disregarding its shame, and has taken his seat at the right hand of the throne of God. (Heb. 12:1-2)

If the world hates us as it hated him, then he is the model of inner joy and blessedness that we ought always to have in mind when we face persecution for righteousness' sake.

Father Joseph Girzone, a retired Roman Catholic priest, has given us a wonderful portrait of Jesus in his novels *Joshua* and *Joshua and the Children*, where Jesus (whose Hebrew name was Yeshua or Joshua) appears in contemporary settings and goes about doing good and getting into trouble. Father Girzone's Joshua is an innately faultless man who by the very fact of his innocence and guilelessness provokes some people into attitudes of defiance and acts of hatred. When he does a good deed, there are usually people who find fault with it. When he speaks the truth, there are those who inevitably take exception to it. He doesn't go about *trying* to upset the *status quo* or bring out the worst in others; it merely happens, as though there must always be an equal and opposite reaction to everything in the moral world as well as in the physical world.

Several people in *Joshua* have become irritated with the way Joshua has talked openly about the meaning of freedom and how some churches have imposed such restrictions on their members that the members are not much better off than the Jewish people were under the rule of the Pharisees. One day as he walks down the street a group of them who are "middle-aged, mostly Catholic, intensely conservative, and deeply distressed about the radical changes taking place in the Church" are poised to confront him in the street. They tell him how unhappy they are with his remarks. He remains calm and gentle, and restates for them his position, especially with regard to the Roman

125

Catholic Church. "What Jesus intended to be so casual and free-spirited," he says, "they have encased in rigid rituals on scheduled times, as if the Holy Spirit worked on timetables dictated by humans."

"So what we have heard is true," retorts a bespectacled man in his mid-forties. "You are hateful of the Church and you criticize her teachings and her laws."

"That is not true," says Joshua.

> "I love the Church, as Jesus loves the Church. It is his great gift to mankind, but there is a human aspect of the Church that needs constant correction and prodding to remain faithful to the spirit of Jesus. Mature Christians should not be afraid to speak their minds and out of real loyalty insist that the spirit of Jesus be followed. They are not servants in a household. They are the family itself, no less than those who like to rule. Jesus wanted his shepherds to be servants, not rulers, and the Christian people should not be afraid to speak. I say what I have said because I care that the Church be what Jesus intended it to be, a haven of peace, and a consoling beacon lighting the way, not a prison of the spirit or a sword that cuts and wounds." (New York: Macmillan Publishing Co., 1983, p. 125)

The people become very angry. One woman wants to slap Joshua in the face. Another expresses sorrow for the state of his soul and promises to pray for him. One of the men pronounces him a heretic and promises to do everything in his power to destroy his influence in the community.

Joshua shakes his head as the group walks away, enraged with him. He remembers the scribes and Pharisees in the first century, and how they couldn't comprehend what the Father was trying to do in his world.

Later, as the conflict deepens, someone asks Joshua the secret of his unearthly peace and contentment, that allows him to live amidst turmoil and hatred as if he had an inner gyroscope forever set on the twin poles of love and understanding.

> "My peace comes from within," Joshua told them. "The simplicity of my life reflects what I possess inside. . . . I do not let myself be hurt by events. I realize all humanity is in a process of

126

growing and, of necessity, will always be imperfect. It can never be any different. I understand that and accept it, and love people for what they are, and I find them enjoyable because our Father made them that way. Find God and learn to love people, and you will find the same peace and harmony with nature." (*Joshua*, p. 151)

This is why Jesus said the blessedness of the persecuted is now as well as in some future time.

The peace is inside. It is not something to be given at a later date. It is here now.

It is a gift of God to all disciples.

CHAPTER NINE

LETTING GOD BLESS YOU

I met the man at a Texas-style reception. He had a smile on his face half-a-mile wide. I asked what made him so radiant.

"My wife left me," he said.

I had known some men who might have rejoiced if their wives left them, but none so blatantly as this, I thought.

"I lost my job," the man continued.

Well, I thought, some jobs might make you feel that way if you lost them.

"Then I lost a second job," he said.

I began to think the man was a nut. He was still grinning from ear to ear.

"I had to let my house go back to the bank," he said.

Still smiling. Now I knew he was a nut.

"My life was simply terrible," he said. "Then I learned how to let God bless me, and it turned everything around."

He told me how he had hit rock bottom in his life, with no money, no family, and no prospects, and then how he had redis-covered his faith in God. "As long as God was with me," he said, "the other things didn't matter so much. Oh, they mattered. I can't pretend they didn't. But they weren't devastating. I learned to see the good things around me all the time. I began thanking God for my health and the sunshine and all the people I met. Pretty soon, I was feeling on top of everything. And you know, when I felt that way, I really *was* on top. My whole life began to blossom! That's why I'm so happy."

I thought about the man as I flew home the next day.

I thought about God.

It is God's nature to bless. That is part of what the Beatitudes are all about. People think they have to set up elaborate religious systems to please God and then jump through spiritual hoops all their lives. But the truth is that God has always wanted to bless us just the way we are, if we are only open to his love and willing to live peaceably and caringly with the other persons around us.

God has always been a blesser. He created the world out of his own happiness. He blessed Adam and Eve and told them to enjoy the world. He blessed Abraham and Moses and David. He blessed the prophets. He blessed Jesus and the Apostles. He has always had his hands open to give people love and life and joy if they could only receive them.

Jesus knew this. He saw it in spite of all the tough things that happened to him. This is why he went to the cross with such equanimity and composure. He had peace in his heart because he could see the fundamental nature of God and what God was doing to usher in the age of the anti-structures, the divine rule that would one day take the place of all the failed structures of ordinary human society.

What Jesus perceived was our fundamental childship with God—the fact that we are sons and daughters of the Most High, the Ultimate Good, the Final Power. Therefore it was not the scribes and Pharisees who were going to be first in the Kingdom, in the time of God's eternal reign, but the simple folks, the ones who were poor in spirit, who felt grief for what they had lost, who were meek and lowly, with servant attitudes, who hungered for righteousness in the world, who showed mercy and generosity to others, who were pure in their hearts, who lived as peacemakers, contributing to the greater welfare of humanity, and who, because they were innocent and good, tended to suffer at the hands of those who were powerful and evil.

The man from Texas was right. God wants to bless us. God wants our world to be a good and happy place. We just need to start seeing the world that way and to stop trying to struggle with it in our own power. If we could only view things the way Jesus did, it would make all the difference in the way we are able to live.

It is so simple that many people miss it. God is not trying to get us to do a lot of things, said Jesus. We don't have to stop being human in order to become religious. All we need to do is remember one thing: To make the kingdom of God and his righteousness the most central thing in our lives (Matt. 6:33). If we will do this, said Jesus, everything else will fall into place. We'll live simply and happily, with all our values and ambitions in order. We won't live anxiously, wanting things we don't have and worrying about the things we can't do. Life will unfold naturally and beautifully, and we will see God's hand in everything that happens.

The Gospels are filled with corroborations of this principle. Take, for example, the story of Jesus' visit to the home of his friends Mary and Martha (Luke 10:38-42). The Scriptures make the point that it was Martha who received Jesus. That is, she is the one who invited him and then felt the responsibility to look after him when he had come. She may have had a type A personality—aggressive, take-charge, competitive, eager to succeed at whatever she undertook.

But Mary, her sister, was there. It was her home, too. And she took advantage of the Master's presence. While Martha busied herself with the servant's role, perhaps cleaning, cooking, preparing a place for Jesus to sleep, Mary simply sat at Jesus' feet and listened to him as he taught.

The fact that Jesus was teaching indicates that there were probably a number of people present. Martha had invited her friends and neighbors so Jesus could talk to them about his work and the coming rule of God. Thus she had a great deal of work to do, seeing that everyone was cared for and the meeting ran smoothly.

In the course of things, Martha became upset with Mary, who was enjoying all the benefits of Jesus' visit but having to do nothing to pay for it. She came to Jesus and said, "Lord, do you not care that my sister has left me to serve alone? Tell her then to help me."

We understand her feelings, don't we?

We would be miffed too.

But what did Jesus say to Martha?

"Martha, Martha, you are anxious and troubled about many things; one thing is needful. Mary has chosen the good portion, which shall not be taken away from her" (Luke 10:41-42).

"Anxious and troubled"—perhaps recalling his words in the Sermon on the Mount, "Do not be anxious" (Matt. 6:25 RSV), or what he said to the disciples at the Last Supper, "Do not let your hearts be troubled" (John 14:1).

Why not anxious and troubled? Because only "one thing is needful."

What is that?

"Seek first his kingdom and his righteousness."

Is that the one thing needful? It would seem to be. Mary has chosen it, and it can't be taken away from her. She is calm and composed at the feet of Jesus, while Martha bustles about, perspiring and anxious over everything and everybody. Mary knows how to let God bless her, by simply being herself and sitting at the feet of her Master.

And what about Jesus' story of the prodigal son (Luke 15:11-32)? That, too, is about the way to find blessedness, isn't it?

The father in the story is a real blesser.

First, he gives the adventurous young son a share of his property. He doesn't have to do that. It is certainly counter to what we might expect of a father in the first century. When the son asked for the money, he might well have laughed in the son's face and sent him to the fields to hoe out the weeds. But apparently he is a gentle, thoughtful father. And generous. He divides what he has with him.

The son goes away. He doesn't think he needs the father any more, now that he has money. He packs himself off to a foreign country and establishes a high style of living for himself.

But it doesn't last. He didn't earn the money and he doesn't know how to take care of it. There isn't much rain for a couple of years and the country is suddenly gripped by a huge famine. Food prices double, triple, quadruple. The young man's money runs out. He can't even feed himself.

Desperate, he enters the employ of a pig farmer and is put to work slopping hogs.

It is despicable work, especially for a Jewish boy. All day long, pushing carts of bean pods out into the fields among the grunting, rooting hogs.

And he is so hungry that he would like to eat the pods himself. Maybe he does even try to chew up some of them, tough as they are.

And one day he has a moment of self-actualization. He sees his true condition.

"My God!" he thinks to himself. "What an irony! Here I am pushing these cartloads of pods to the pigs, while the hired servants on my father's land sit down to plenty." At his father's house, the blessedness of the father extends like an aura to everyone around, even the servants. The son has unfortunately removed himself from the father's environment; he is beyond the pale of the father's blessings.

This peak experience he has had leads to a new resolution, a new way of seeing what he can do to remedy his dire situation. "I will arise and go to my father," he resolves, "and I will say to him, 'Father, I have sinned against heaven and before you; I am no longer worthy to be called your son; treat me as one of your hired servants'" (Luke 15:18-19 RSV).

From his present perspective, the blessings of a servant would be very sufficient. He doesn't dream of being restored to sonship. Taking his inheritance has been tantamount to treating his father as if he were dead. The most he can hope for is to be hired on like the other servants.

So he goes back home, dreaming low.

And the father surprises him. Does he *ever* surprise him! He begins lavishing blessings on the son, the way he always did. Maybe even more than before.

"Bring quickly the best robe," he tells the servants, "and put it on him; and put a ring on his hand, and shoes on his feet; and bring the fatted calf and kill it, and let us eat and make merry; for this my son was dead, and is alive again; he was lost, and is found" (Luke 15:22-24 RSV).

All those blessings—a new robe, a ring, shoes, a party with a fatted calf, and sonship. It's dazzling, isn't it? If you're accustomed to saying "wow," it makes you want to say, "Wow! Did he ever bless him!"

The son doesn't do anything but come home and ask to be a servant. He doesn't bring any gifts. He can't; he doesn't have any money. He probably doesn't even look very good; otherwise he wouldn't need a new robe and shoes. He just comes back and presents himself, and it is enough. The father blesses him.

What does this say about our relationship to God? That we have to work very hard to please God? That we have to keep all the rules and always go to Sunday school and church and never abuse drugs and alcohol? That we have to read our Bibles every day and pray at least half an hour in the morning or evening and never forget to say grace over our meals?

No. We only have to come into the Father's presence. Then it begins. The blessings start to fall upon us. And the biggest blessing of all is being God's child again. It's wonderful.

Now, the father wants to bless the elder son too, the one who stays at home all the time and never does anything to cause his father embarrassment.

"Son," he says, "everything I have is yours."

But the elder son can't see it. Something in his attitude restricts him. He can't open his hands—or his heart—and take the blessings.

He envies the openness of his younger brother. He resents the easy way this brother simply comes back and relates to their father as if he hasn't been away at all. He protests to the father. His brother, he says, has been a disgrace, using up the father's money with harlots.

"That isn't the right attitude," the father says. "Your brother was dead, for all we know, and he's come back to life. He was lost to us, and we've found him again. We should rejoice and have a good time. This is something to celebrate!"

But the poor elder son cannot enter into the merriment. He figures he's been cheated. He has the mind of an accountant, and he has been keeping score on everyone. He is very unhappy.

Isn't this the way it is with a lot of us? We can't accept the happiness. We know we don't deserve it, or that something will happen to take it away. Or if it's a matter of others' happiness, we know they don't deserve it either. They *especially* don't deserve it.

So we just keep struggling and contending for everything. We turn life into a contest or a combat zone. We have to keep proving ourselves, time after time, year after year. We can't merely relax and accept the joy and the happiness. We are like old Ebenezer Scrooge before his conversion—we want life to be earnest and hard and unrelenting.

We *make* life earnest and hard and unrelenting.

It's strange, isn't it, how some people are able to relax and accept the blessings of life while others continue to fight and struggle all their lives? Jesus was a wise man. He knew that even within the same family one child can accept blessings and the other can't. One son revels in it, while the other rejects it.

Wouldn't you like to be a person who finds blessings everywhere and lives positively all the time?

We have a friend who was raped a couple of years ago. Many people who are raped feel stigmatized by it the rest of their lives. The experience of being raped becomes the focal point of their existence, so that eventually everything circulates around it.

But our friend is different.

"I will not be victimized by what has happened to me," she says. "It was only a moment in my life. I will not let it *become* my life."

She talks openly about the experience. Her positive, radiant attitude has become a watchword in her community. It is a godsend to other women who undergo similar experiences. They are learning from her that life is not sullied by a single occasion when it is compromised. She still sees the blessings around her. She lives with a song in her voice. She knows there is plenty of evil in the world around her, but she will not permit it to set up camp in her mind.

I believe this is where the power of positive thinking and science-of-the-mind concepts are right. A person's attitude is all-important. How we look at life makes a difference in how happy we are and what comes to us in the course of a lifetime. It would have been perfectly easy for our friend to succumb to the undertow of her experience. But she did not. She is a happy, upbeat person. She is a strong Christian, and her beliefs about the rule of God form the undergirding for a wonderful outlook on life. "I will not let this thing beat me," she said, "or take from me the joys of life." And she didn't.

We have another friend, a man in his late sixties. He is one of the most cheerful, outgoing people I ever met. When he walks into a room, it lights up with the glow on his face.

He told me once what his secret is.

"I'm a Christian," he said, "and that influences everything I feel and do. If something bad or awkward happens to me, I immediately look for the other side of it. I ask, 'How is God going to bless me through what has just happened?' For example, if I have a flat tire, I pull off the highway, give thanks to God for the accident it has probably helped me avert, fix the tire, and go on. If I make a *faux pas* in a social setting, I say, 'Thank you, Lord, for what I just did; maybe it made somebody else more comfortable so they can relate to me.' Whatever it is, it has a good side. Otherwise what Paul said to the Romans wouldn't be true, that 'we know that all things work together for good for those who love God, who are called according to his purpose' " (Rom. 8:28).

I can't think about this man without having a smile on my face. He leads a blessed existence because he is always looking for God's blessings.

We now know, of course, that even a person's health is often determined by how he or she looks at life. An article in the *Los Angeles Times* reported on a ten-year study made by researchers at Stanford University and the University of California at Berkeley of women with metastatic breast cancer. Dr. David Spiegel, reporting on the study to the American Psychiatric Association, said that he was frankly "quite stunned" by what the researchers found. He had expected their study to refute the notion that the right mental attitude can help to conquer disease; as a scientist, he was not prepared for anything else. But what the study showed is that cancer patients receiving emotional support from others and having a good mental attitude toward their ailment often survive up to twice as long as other patients exhibiting a poor mental attitude.

There is an example of this right now on our university campus. The wife of one of the administrators was diagnosed with terminal cancer almost three years ago. At that time, the doctors said she had perhaps six months to live. But they were dealing only with the medical side of her condition. They were not counting on the great faith and happiness of the woman and her husband. "God has been wonderful to us," they said, "and he will not stop being wonderful because of this cancer."

They continued to live normal, active lives, which for them, included prayer and Bible study every day. She made several trips to another state to visit her children and grandchildren. Once, she even made a trip to Europe to visit a child who lived there. The trips tire her, but she continues to pray and to go. She is one of the loveliest, most radiant people I have ever known. Everyone marvels at her gentle tenacity and unwavering faith. But of course the gentle tenacity comes from the unwavering faith. She is coexisting so beautifully with the cancer in her body because she knows that God is a God of blessedness, and she has that blessedness in her heart.

Let's return to Jesus' parable.

Here is a young man who loses all his money and comes close to starvation. But he has a positive mental attitude. He thinks about his father's house and how even the servants there have fared well. He doesn't beat himself for having gone into the far country. He doesn't complain because he lost all his money. He simply says, "I will arise and go to my father and ask to be one of his hired hands."

He isn't going to stand on formality.

He isn't going to live as a martyr to what has happened to him.

He knows the world is still full of blessings and he is going to go where he knows a few of them will fall his way.

His older brother, by contrast, is right there with the source of blessings all the time, yet never seems to realize it. He sees his younger brother, when he comes home, getting a lot of attention. Instead of recognizing that he has enjoyed the same attention for years, he becomes jealous of his brother. His life is all choked up with envy and hatred. He can't see the blessings that cluster around him like grapes on the vine.

What it all comes down to is that God is a God of blessings— fantastic blessings—and wants to bestow these blessings on us with a free hand. God has already bestowed them upon us, in fact; our lives are steeped in them, even if we are poor or in mourning, even if we are humble and starved for righteousness, even if we are among those under persecution for righteousness' sake. Only some of us are unable to see the blessedness because of our poor mental attitudes. When we aren't focused on the coming rule of God, on the ultimate glorification of the Crucified One and all his followers, we get everything out of perspective and forget to be thankful. We are as blind and self-tormented as the elder brother.

Jesus didn't say, "Blessed are the rich" and "Blessed are those who never look back" and "Blessed are those who take what they want" and "Blessed are the corrupt in heart, who understand how to get along in the world." He said "Blessed are the poor," "Blessed are those who mourn," "Blessed are the meek," "Blessed are the pure in heart."

Even when we are in the most abject condition, God is there blessing us.

It's a "win-win" situation all the way!

There is one more thing.

People who manage to stay focused on God's reign, and thus to see the blessings around them, are also the ones most open to sharing their blessings with others. I have watched this for a lifetime, and I know it is true. Those with a positive attitude, who know that the world is a garden of blessedness, live with a free and easy attitude toward the riches God sends their way.

This is the way Jesus told his disciples to live. When he sent them out to preach the arrival of the reign of God, he said, "You have received without payment, give without payment" (Matt. 10:8). The blessings of the kingdom had come freely and openly to them, without their expecting them or having to perform any special duties to receive them; they were to pass them on as freely and openly to others, reveling in the fact that they were conduits, channels of the heavenly gifts.

This is a Kingdom attitude, you see. It comes from realizing that God owns the world and bestows his blessings freely on everyone. All the disciple needs to do is realize this and hold out his or her hands, both to receive and to give.

I know a beautiful woman who is ninety years old and has always been extremely generous with everything she has. She helps foreign students who want to come to this country to study. She sends flowers and food to people who have had a distressing time of any kind. She gives frequent dinners and parties in order to be able to introduce people to one another. Often she sends theater and concert tickets to people she knows would appreciate them but can't afford to buy them. She is always doing something nice for somebody or giving somebody something he or she needs. Everyone loves her because of her selflessness and generosity.

I said to her one day, "You are so good to everybody."

"Oh no," she said, "it is God who has been good to me. He has given me so much more than I can ever use. The more I give away, the more I have. It is wonderful!"

She is a channel. God uses her to bless others because she doesn't restrict what is given to her. She is open to others and lets the blessings flow through her to the world. And she is happy because she is at the point of intersection where God's gifts reach the others who need them. She sits at the crossroads and enjoys everything!

If there is a final message in this book, then, it is this: Permit God to bless you.

Don't look around you and think how hard life is. Look around and see how filled with mystery and goodness it is. See how wonderful the world looks when you know God is at work redeeming it and setting up the anti-structures, so that humility and purity and compassion and longing for justice and peace will all be fulfilled and rewarded in the eternal scheme of things.

Give thanks to God for the richness of existence.

Then look around to see who you can share it with.

That will make you even richer.

If you will learn to live this way every day, you will always have a song in your heart and the path before you will be lined with flowers. Joy will spring up inside you like a fountain, and you will lie down to sleep at night with peace in your soul. And you will say, "Blessed be the name of our God forever and ever, who calls us to a new rule where righteousness will be the order of the day forever!"